Jobless

Loving What You Do

Lucille H. Freeman

LUCILLE USHER FREEMAN

CAROUSEL
LEGENDS PRESS, INC

Copyright ©2020 Lucille Usher Freeman
Carousel Legends Press, Inc.

All rights reserved. No part of this publication may be reproduced, stored in a retrieval system or transmitted in any form or by any means, electronic, mechanical, including photocopying, recording or otherwise without prior written consent from the publisher.

Scripture marked NKJV taken from the New King James Version®. Copyright © 1982 by Thomas Nelson. Used by permission. All rights reserved.

Scripture quotations marked NLT are taken from the Holy Bible, New Living Translation, copyright © 1996, 2004, 2015 by Tyndale House Foundation. Used by permission of Tyndale House Publishers, Inc., Carol Stream, Illinois 60188. All rights reserved.

ISBN 978-1-950733-01-9

Acknowledgements

To my birth family and family of the heart: Roberta Fields, Patricia Holder, Robert Holder Jr., Derrick Lampkin Sr., Vickie Harris and Henry and Audrey Locke.

To my children and grandkids: I'll love you forever. Deavay Tyler; Kash'shawn Tyler Johnson; Donnavan Paul Tyler, Kelvin Johnson, April Tyler and Kim Tyler. I can't imagine life without you. To Jadyn, Alaina, Chiam, Madison, Journey, Faith, Ranen, Sage, Mikayla, and Ethan. You have made me to know endless sunlight; you brighten my world.

To Dr. Michael Wilkins and Delcine Wilkins, and my SPAA family, thanks for the many ways you have encouraged me to grow.

To my real estate family: Henrine Taylor, Al Staples, Darnelle and Oddette Sanders, Ernestine Barnes, William Rodney and Stephanie Windham, your continued encouragement and acceptance have inspired me to sprout wings.

To my literary friends: Cynthia Hutson (with a "T"); Tina Bell (let's hear it for FLOW); and my Ragdale family (you inspire me to be and do more); Linda Williams (Ragsdale's chef) you feed us creatives not only food but joy with your smiles and welcoming kitchen. Shelley and C.J. Hitz you have been an infinite source of inspiration to me; may God continue to bless your lives.

To those who have left me a legacy of wisdom: Robert L. Usher, Madora Usher, Pauline Lampkin, Sonya Fields, Ruby L. Oliver, Rubie Stepney and Madearia King. Thanks for investing in me.

To my countless nieces and nephews. Lots of love, keep passing the torch.

To Rachel Ray Moulder, Brenda Miller, Debra Rash, Janet C. Bell, Tonja Guerrero, Rita Mhoon, Iona Johnson, Jeanette Cunningham and Freida Brothers. You've given me many seasons of friendship.

A special thanks to my editor, Nancy Haight and to my formatter, book cover designer and publishing consultant, Katie Erickson.

Like a pastor said in church one day, "I know when I start naming names, I probably will miss someone. Charge it to my head, not my heart."

Finally, God thank you for helping me get through so many challenges and always keeping your promises to help and strengthen me. My faith has been a foundation as I continue to stretch, stay hopeful and to repeatedly put on a coat of courage. Thanks for answering my many jobless prayers.

Disclaimer: While the anecdotes are based on true stories, some of the names have been changed to protect the party's identity.

Table of Contents

Chapter 1: Can I Survive Without a 9-5 Job? 1
Chapter 2: Seeing Yourself Happily Jobless 4
Chapter 3: Thrown into the Jobless Pit 8
Chapter 4: Jobless vs. Work-Less 12
Chapter 5: A Poor Fit 16
Chapter 6: The Courageous Truth 22
Chapter 7: Clock-Watchers 25
Chapter 8: The Jobless Quest 28
Chapter 9: Transformation 32
Chapter 10: God, Take Care of this Goose 37
Chapter 11: No Regrets 43
Chapter 12: Sixteen Tons: Feeling Deserving 49
Chapter 13: Write the Vision 56
Chapter 14: Getting Out of a Job Rut 60
Chapter 15: Facing Obstacles 63
Chapter 16: Power in the Little 69
Chapter 17: Role Models of Success 74
Chapter 18: The Process 79
Chapter 19: Financial Obstacles 83
Chapter 20: Stretch Your Wings 92
Chapter 21: Employing Our Faith 97
Chapter 22: Keep Flying 101
Chapter 23: Jobless Affirmations 105

CHAPTER 1

Can I Survive Without a 9-5 Job?

"A popular bumper sticker reads, 'I owe, I owe, it's off to work I go.' This isn't funny; it's a tragedy! And it's worse than depressing; it's devastating."
- Russ Whitney
Author of <u>Building Wealth</u>

THE LONGING

Do you consistently complain about going to work? Do you struggle each weekend with the Sunday-night blues? Do you hate hearing the alarm clock each morning? *Morning again? Gosh, I can't wait for the weekend!*

Are you caught in a web of huge charge-card balances, a mortgage and the expenses of everyday living? Does the mere thought of searching for a new career render you helpless?

Even if your "job-sentence" ends and you retire, you may ask yourself, "Will I be able to live off only a percentage of my salary when it's hard making ends meet with it all?"

Do you count the minutes until five o'clock and the days and months to your next vacation?

Are you secretly harboring a desire to leave your job or start a business?

Is there a musician, photographer, dancer, entrepreneur or artist hidden inside you, fighting to get out?

Are there books in you but little time and energy to write them?

Is there a longing to trade in your corporate suits to become a full-time mother?

Do you celebrate the jobless—those who pursue their passions, like the Bill Gates, Oprah Winfreys, Warren Buffets, Tyler Perrys of the world—yet reluctantly swipe a time clock each morning?

The real question is: Can you survive without a nine-to-five job?

This book encourages you to answer your inner calling and move towards joblessness. Joblessness does not mean being lazy or unproductive; it means building streams of income doing work you enjoy. This book inspires you to listen to your urgings rather than the fear that says you can't make money doing what you love and are uniquely designed to do.

Be patient and courageous. Earning income in areas of your gifts, purpose and talent, and in ways that feel natural to you, means leaving your comfort zone, which will take effort and time, but in the end, it will be rewarding.

First, it's important to admit that it's time to change direction, because your current job isn't a good fit *now*. We all evolve. Give yourself permission to make the needed changes.

If you find yourself without employment, don't panic; this could be an ideal time to reflect and commit to changing. Truthfulness in face of fear is paramount. It will take courage and planning to get on a ship and head to a new world, with clouds of the unknown, with possible financial storms, and with uncertainty and danger lingering by. Will you heed the voice inside that's been screaming, "You can't stay here!" and commit to a new career journey?

When your current job doesn't feed the essence of who you've become, how do you find work more suited to you?

This book encourages you to stay focused and determined and to jump off that diving board of an ill-fitted job once and for all. Changing careers doesn't have to be an all-or-nothing process; you can sail into your new job horizon gradually. Don't discount the power of little steps and achievements.

One day, you'll wake up to discover that your trip into the unknown has yielded a brand-new world full of amazing mysteries, spices, and possibilities. Adopt a new mindset. Be willing to make the trip.

> *"If you find yourself in a situation you don't like, either work to make it better or leave. Do something to change it or get the heck out. Agree to work on the relationship or get a divorce. Work to improve working conditions or find a new job."*
>
> *- Jack Canfield*
> <u>The Success Principles</u>

CHAPTER 2
Seeing Yourself Happily Jobless

"We're so different from each other that explaining why you love what you love to someone else is like trying to explain opera to a cat."
- *Barbara Sher*
Author of <u>Live the Life You Love</u>

Sandra Lee, a former addiction counselor, refers to her joblessness as a gift she's giving herself to nurture her creative spirit. She wants to pursue writing and has set goals to complete her books and scripts.

Tina Bell referred to her self-imposed joblessness as a season to be a full-time housewife and mother to her four kids.

Cheryl Jackson, a former teacher and divorcee, thrusted herself from the grips of traditional employment to nurture her dreams of owning her own child care center.

Rodessa Joiner and Darnell Sandifer wanted to work in the real estate field, to try their hands at ownership, real estate sales, appraising and property management. The question for them both was, "Can I earn enough money in this field so that I won't have to work a 9 to 5 job?"

For Rachel Moulder, traveling was important—not that two-week vacation that comes once a year for the employed. She wanted to spend three or four months in Florida in the winter time. "Chicago gets pretty cold, but because my grandchildren and family are here, I'm not ready to leave the city entirely."

Others who dream of life without a nine-to-five job cite some of the following reasons.

- "I need time to exercise and to focus on my interests, like art and music."
- "I want to control my own time."
- "I don't want my life to be controlled by an alarm clock."
- "I can't stand the long commutes to work and back. It takes me a total of three to four hours of traveling time each day, depending on the traffic."
- "I hate Mondays and look forward to Fridays. I don't particularly enjoy my job."
- "I want to leave generational wealth, and I can't do it with just a run-of-the mill job."
- "I want to pursue my calling."

A JOBLESS VISION

For Ted Williams, who has worked for over 20 years in the technology industry, retirement or being happily jobless has been a personal goal but not an option for him for several decades. Finally, he can see the finish line, but if he could have seen his way beyond credit card bills, car and mortgage payments and education costs for his two children, he admits he would have opted for a jobless lifestyle or retirement years ago. He's anxious to join the ranks of those happily jobless.

Do you see being without a job as synonymous with a lack of productivity, not being diligent, and worst of all, being poor or broke?

Have you, however, considered that Warren Buffet, Oprah Winfrey, George Lucas and Tyler Perry are diligent but don't show up at a job every day and punch a time clock? Experts say millions, citing from 70 to 80 percent of the population, don't particularly enjoy their jobs, but they feel tied to their work because of financial obligations, citing mortgages for their homes, car notes, credit card payments and the ever increasing cost of living as the reasons why they're anchored to life-draining careers.

For those who defer their dreams of pursuing their callings, decades may pass before they realize retirement doesn't guarantee that time and income will be there to live the happily-after-work lifestyle. Hopefully, the golden years won't find them warring to make ends meet and fighting to protect their health.

With the new direction our digital and technology-driven workplace has taken, fewer people are guaranteed gold watches or blissful retirements, and for many, the American Dream has turned into a nightmare with diminishing 401Ks, mounting personal debt and historical foreclosures and job losses.

When Terry lost his less-than-ideal job, it only took a few weeks for his family to shift into a financial crisis. His wife's Angela's income from a part-time job, which had only been a small portion of the household budget before, moved from being a supplementary part of their household income to their primary income source.

Terry and Angela had lived on Barely-Get-By Street for the past two decades, and they were not prepared for Terry being laid off after receiving a mere two-week notice. Not being armed with an emergency backup fund sent the couple to the brink of financial disaster.

After trying for over a year to get employment in his former industry, Terry and Angela finally decided that perhaps it was time for Terry to pursue a dream he had shelved years ago. Terry and Angela started their own printing company with the last of their savings, help from family members, and an ample number of prayers.

For the first year or two, Terry and Angela struggled to keep the business going. When year four came, Terry realized he was making a moderate salary from the endeavor.

By year six, Terry found himself among the blissfully jobless. After all, he did not consider doing what he loved a job but rather a dream come true. He had traded in the long commutes, suits, ties, and office politics for a chance to be productive and to make an income. He even considered that perhaps the business could become part of his family legacy, giving his sons a chance to experience entrepreneurship and break out of the barely-get-by existence that he and his wife had lived in for years.

Although Terry had not entirely fulfilled all his financial goals, he was enjoying freedom, life and his work in a way he could have never imagined.

"If you find success in your career, you will look forward to every day with a 'T.G.I.T.' mentality: 'Thank God It's Today!' Then Monday will become your most exciting day of the week, because it means that you can go back to doing the things you love to do and get paid to do them!"
- Dwight Bain
Author of Destination Success:
A Map for Living Out Your Dreams

Chapter 3

Thrown into the Jobless Pit

"Change that's inflicted on you is not necessarily bad."
- Marti Smye
Consultant, speaker and author of books including <u>Is It Too Late to Run Away and Join the Circus?</u>

When the coronavirus hit, employees nationwide found themselves unexpectedly jobless; the unemployment lines and calls to the unemployment center were record-breaking. Although authorities and politicians promised to fix the issue, they acknowledge they had never seen anything like the record number of job losses in history.

Personally, my heart went out to those who were fighting the pandemic while facing big issues, like feeding their families and paying their housing and car bills. A freeze was placed on evictions, foreclosures and shutting off utilities, but the freeze wasn't going to last forever, just like the coronavirus.

Businesses closed in record numbers, and the stock market plummeted, and the country's economy was heavily hit. We were brought to our knees. Prayers were hitting the airwaves since churches could no longer assemble, and many were seeing the need to pray for themselves and for our land.

Truly, it was a situation beyond our control; the coronavirus pandemic, a world-wide disease and crisis, caused mandatory shutdowns and quarantines.

Throughout the years, people have found themselves unemployed, and many times, the reason was beyond their control, such as down-sizings, industry shake-ups, corporate house cleaning and business closings. It creates emotional chaos when you are forced to join the ranks of the unemployed. Still, when faced with this dilemma, preparation and attitude are paramount.

"It's terrible—one of the worst things that could have happened. I didn't save or plan for this moment," Jeff said. "My first question was, *how will I survive?* I had house payments, a wife, children and car notes. How could I make it?"

On the other hand, Nate, another man looking from a different perspective, said, "I hadn't been happy in my job for some years. I was a bad fit for it, and it was a bad fit for me. Yes, it was challenging, but joblessness gave me a chance to see where I was. Who knows, maybe I'll start my own business."

Both men qualified for unemployment benefits. While one man perched on the edge of fear and hopelessness, the other man decided this would never happen to him again and chose to leap towards entrepreneurship, looking at his season of joblessness as a gift. Although Nate felt there was not much he could do about the pandemic and applied for unemployment compensation while waiting for a government stimulus check, he promised never to be caught without rainy-day resources again. With little chance of ever returning to his former job, Nate also decided to search for employment, but he finally began pursuing his dreams of entrepreneurship too.

As Robert Allen's book and the scripture reminds us, it's all about, *As a man thinketh.* One man sees joblessness as a disaster while another sees joblessness as his road to freedom and a brighter future.

THE GIFTS OF JOBLESSNESS

When forced into joblessness, there are many struggles and obstacles to overcome, but there are gifts as well. If you are so overwhelmed by your immediate financial needs, you may be blinded to the opportunities that exist. When the season of unemployment comes with a severance package or an unemployment check, this can actually be a gift to give you time and resources to seek employment or self-employment in an area of your true calling.

For you, joblessness could mean an opportunity to explore career changes, return to school, move to a different location, or pursue changing a hobby or passion into a money-making venture. While some may see the gift in joblessness, others may approach sudden unemployment with a sense of fear, believing that a steady job is the only means to a steady income.

What if being booted out of the workplace, armed with a severance package and possibly future unemployment checks, becomes your motivating force for seeking a more fulfilling career? Or maybe it will become the catalyst for you to start your own business. What if the frustration of being let go becomes a *golden ticket* to building a stream of income that doesn't feel like work but like an opportunity to pursue your purpose while forever changing your life direction? Even when you are thrown into the jobless pit, remember that opportunities are often disguised as problems.

LOVING WHAT YOU DO

Considering the exuberant amount of time our careers demand—preparing for work, commuting to the workplace or just being at the job—why not spend the time in a job uniquely suited to you and to your likes and tastes? Why not actually enjoy the work you spend most of your waking hours engaged in? Why not strive for job satisfaction?

When you enjoy your job, it takes most of the work out of it and puts it into the category of passion and play. Welcome to a book that encourages you to find your jobless self. It is in the state of being jobless that you will produce a more powerful income, cater to your interests and talents, and design a life tailored to who you are. Welcome to the ranks of the jobless.

Rather than seeing a layoff as a disaster or as an insurmountable problem, re-frame to see it as an opportunity. Make up your mind that you will swim and not sink. Take the challenge by the reins, and refuse to be a victim or to talk victim talk. Remember you are powerful and gifted; let strength be the guiding light as you pursue employment or entrepreneurship.

For many who have not only lost jobs but loved ones as well, as the thief of coronavirus has forever altered our lives, this season could become a cry to answer your heart's desire, to not be entrapped by fear or work drudgery and to passionately live the life you've been given.

It has been a very sad wake-up call for us all.

"Repeatedly I hear from people eighteen months after they were fired that losing their jobs was 'the best thing that ever happened' to them."
- Dan Miller
Author of <u>No More Mondays</u>

Chapter 4
Jobless Vs. Work-Less

"If you ask me, the reason five out of ten people in this country hate their jobs and 17 million are clinically depressed is that they're leading lives that are 'way beneath them.' They're exhausting themselves on meaningless things."

- Pamela Grout
Author of Living Big

My dad worked full-time at the post office for 40 years, while simultaneously working his part-time job at a local retail store for 25 years. When I shared my goal of leaving my teaching job to venture into entrepreneurship, he said, "You're my lazy child."

My plans to pursue a job and income outside the traditional workplace were not on my dad's radar. My father believed making an income was much more important than liking the job you were required to do to earn the income. Even though I didn't buy into his beliefs, I appreciated that he was willing to be self-sacrificing when it came to providing for my mom and his four daughters. Doing something he loved was probably an idea he rarely entertained, if he considered it at all. Maybe he considered changing careers a bit risky and a risk he wasn't willing to take and subject his family to.

I knew my dad loved me, even though my dreams of self-employment were met with negativity. My parents, who did not have college degrees, considered teaching a prime job and one with status.

Teaching, they thought, didn't require a lot of physical energy, and my mom often referred to being an educator as a "pencil pusher" job, not requiring a lot of menial work. My parents didn't understand that itch inside me that pointed me towards entrepreneurship and answering the call to do what I loved. My sisters, friends, colleagues and others in my immediate circle saw my urge for independence and for not punching a time clock as a form of me harboring a complaining and unappreciative attitude.

Instead of adapting the attitude of those around me or expecting support, I often turned away from my immediate circle, broadening my sphere of influence to include other business people, such as my an aunt, who was an entrepreneur, and people who knew making an income through entrepreneurship was not an impossible dream because they were doing it themselves.

At times, rather than putting my dreams up for criticism, I remembered the biblical story of Joseph, who told his brothers about his dreams and was thrown into the pit. I learned the power of silence and became picky about whom I shared my entrepreneur goals with. My self-help books spoke about dream-killers, and I didn't want to subject my dreams to those murderers.

LEAVING THE WORK BARREL

Do you have a limiting belief about what it means to be jobless? Maybe your birth-family, your friends and your community have passed on the notion that *not* having a job promotes laziness and *not* having a traditional job signals that you are slothful. Perhaps, within your circle, when people have tried to escape the clutches of 9-to-5 living, they've been incorrectly labeled, and it was predicated that they would fail. Like the crabs-in-the-barrel syndrome, some friends and even family members want you to stay in the work barrel for your own safety and because of their own limited beliefs. After all, what good can come to someone who doesn't opt for traditional employment? They can't see their way out of the barrel and so, it's an act of protection. It's for your own good.

Note, however, there is a huge difference between being without a job and being unproductive. Often parents tell children coming out of college that their job is to find a job. For some reason, maybe because of the mountain of school loans or maybe they fear the child will be a life-long non-working student, parents often fail to add the word "right" to the word job. "You should find the *right* job."

Consider this: not having a job is not the same as being idle; some of the most diligent people in the world, some of the most productive...and wealthiest...are jobless.

When your work becomes your play and your play becomes your work, you too will be jobless. I've known that I'm not a traditional nine-to-fiver since I was a teenager. Although I worked a traditional job for years, since high school, I've had a jobless spirit and have always moved towards the joblessness I am enjoying today.

For some, there's an urge to work independently to become an entrepreneur, artist, writer, musician, actor or actress and to work outside the boundaries and restrictions of the conventional workplace. If that rings true to you, maybe you too have been called outside the traditional workplace.

Working a job can be a bad fit for someone whose creative spirit continually fights for freedom. You can be—as the childhood story goes—an ugly "work" duckling. Perhaps you are an eagle, pecking away in the barnyard, watching the other eagles fly overhead and wondering when you will be able to break away and fly towards a career more suited to you.

What do you have to break away from? Conventional thoughts, traditional people, the soothsayers of negativity? Do you need to avoid people who say, "You can't, and if you try, you will be doomed to homeliness and poverty without a job!" It is difficult when those discouraging you are your friends, relatives or someone you love, whose minds have been trained by the standard educational and work systems. I sometimes wonder, how many owners of the Fortune 500 companies are telling their children to just get a job and work it for the next 25 or 35 years?

Walking away from the security (or should we say insecurity) of a job means, like the ending to the *Truman Show*, walking off the set into the darkness of the unknown.

Being jobless doesn't mean being direction-less, goal-less, or penniless, as some might imply.

Joblessness is not an excuse for being lazy. Many of our greatest entrepreneurs work long hard hours, only they work in the arena of their choice and therefore are some of the most diligent people around.

The scriptures say that the hands of the diligent shall rule. Who is as productive as one who can give out of their gifts and talents, interests and strengths? Thus, joblessness and work-less are truly on opposite ends of the globe.

> *"A long time ago someone told me, 'If you do what you love, you never work a day in your life.' In my eyes, there's no truer saying. When you love your work, it doesn't feel like work. It doesn't tax you. It's not overwhelming. It's not a burden. It's something you absolutely, wholeheartedly love."*
>
> *- Tyler Perry*
> *Actor, film-producer and author of books, including* <u>Higher Is Waiting</u>

CHAPTER 5
A Poor Fit

"You are here to create the good, the beautiful, and the holy. You're here to dance, to spread love, to write symphonies, to give birth to the very best that is inside of you. You are here on this planet to love big. To think big thoughts, to dream big dreams.... You've squandered your power on meaningless things. You've bartered it away for security. You've wasted your talent by not trusting it. You've hidden your individuality for a paycheck."
- Pamela Grout
Author of Living Big

GPS devices are able to determine the position of a car, truck or person. I use my GPS system through an app on my phone; it can help take me from where I am to where I want to go. When I think about my inner GPS, I remember what I've often heard minister, entrepreneur and motivational speaker Dr. Mike Murdock say: "A bird doesn't desire to go south unless there is a south to go to."

If there's an urge to travel in a different direction, it's there for a reason. It's a calling, something that points to your purpose, something that should not be ignored. To remain employed in a field that doesn't support who you uniquely are requires you to disconnect from your inner urgings and your inner GPS system. But, resisting your gut-feeling and silencing your inner-voice will eventually lead you to a life of frustration, a lack of fulfillment and regrets.

Often, your inner GPS will beckon you to venture outside your comfort zone, to face your fears and self-doubts. You ask yourself, can I really make a lucrative income in writing, music, dancing, speaking, or comedy? Can I really earn a living in the area of my talent or gifts? Uncertainty visits when you explore the possibilities outside your comfort zone.

There's a scripture on my office wall that says, "For with God all things are possible." Like many, I don't think I've reached high enough to even come close to what's possible for me. It's important to come to terms with venturing outside your comfort zone. I often say, you have to get comfortable with being uncomfortable.

When I look around, things that seemed impossible merely a few decades ago have become a part of my everyday living. Cell phones, Apple watches, digital movies, traveling by airplane, going into outer space, refrigerators and personal computers were at one time far beyond the scope of many of our dreams. So, I ask you, what's possible or what's impossible? Maybe it's time for you to change your set-point. Dream bigger, think higher, reach for more, put on your mountain climbing shoes and your coat of courage and get moving. Remember, every day you live with what was once deemed *impossible*. Each day, you are called beyond your boundaries to venture outside what's comfortable for you.

The realm of impossibility only exists in your mind, the way you think, the world you envision for yourself. It is the cages that we have put ourselves in, which we have refused to leave, that are the real problems. In his book *Instinct*, mega-pastor T. D. Jakes does an excellent job explaining why we remain in our cages.

"Cages are comfortable. Cages are consistent. They provide security. And generally, they are safe."

There are times we ignore our inner guidance system telling us to make a U-turn, to go in a different direction and to veer off course. Instead, we stay in our cages.

THE LION AND THE ELEPHANT

There's a frequently told tale about a lion, the king of the jungle, who is put in captivity, but after some years, the lion-keeper decides to set the lion loose. He takes the lion back to the jungle and opens the cage then stands back to watch. The lion paces back and forth, refusing to leave the cage. The lion-keeper decides to prod the lion from the cage. The lion paces back and forth, as though it is still within the cage's perimeter. The lion-keeper realizes the real problem: although the lion is no longer in the cage, the cage is in him. What cages do you limit yourself to? What thoughts imprison you?

Now consider elephants, one of the largest animals in the world. An adult male elephant weighs between 9 and 14 thousand pounds. A female elephant weighs less, between 6 and 8 thousand pounds. Yet when an elephant is young, it is taught to remain in captivity; a chain and stake is tied to its leg. When the elephant ages and weighs thousands of pounds, it doesn't even attempt to escape and can still be held in place with that same little chain and stake.

What's the chain and stake you're tied to in the employment arena? Do you feel it's impossible to do what you love and to get paid for it? Yes, I am suggesting that perhaps the cage and the stake are merely in your mind.

There are a million ways to earn a million dollars, but only a handful of ideal ways for you to earn your "right livelihood." What is your right livelihood? It is your

> *purpose path--earning money doing things that you truly enjoy to serve all of humanity. The secrets of your right livelihood are already planted inside you.*
> *- Robert Allen and Mark Victor Hansen*
> *Authors of <u>Cash in a Flash: Fast Money in Slow Times</u>*

LAUNCHING: FINDING THE RIGHT LIVELIHOOD

Too much time is spent preparing for your job, thinking about your job, commuting to and from your job and actually being physically present on your job for you to be discontent with your job. Are you silencing your soul's cry and squelching your burning desire to change jobs, because of lack of self-trust or fears? Have you ever asked yourself, "Can I survive without a traditional job?" only to dismiss the thought as not even an option?

If the secrets to your right livelihood are inside, have you ever really looked? Are you afraid of what you might find? How long will you continue to ignore the voice shouting, "I can't keep doing this!" as you prepare for work each day?

As a writer, I am a treasure-chest of stories. I value stories and sometimes, when watching television or a movie, I tend to analyze stories. I see what works and what doesn't, and I try to find the wisdom the tale holds.

As I struggled to leave my traditional job, I would sometimes make a run for it, thinking this is it, yet after launching, I'd find myself back on the ground. Lift has to overcome drag for a plane to take off. And some of the things dragging me back to the arms of a job that was no longer suited for me were my responsibilities, not being financially prepared, not knowing exactly what I would do after leaving, the possibility of no health insurance and worst of all, an underlying layer of fear.

After watching me make several attempts to launch out of a traditional job, my daughter Kash'shawn told me I reminded her of the *Chicken Run* story. This little chicken was so determined to leave the barnyard, but his plans were thwarted. He was recaptured or for some unforeseen reason, he found himself back in the barnyard; still, he never gave up hope. Eventually, he escaped the barnyard and found his freedom. What stood out was the chicken's determination and persistence.

My friend Janet Bell suggested I watch the movie *The Truman Show* because leaving the familiar can be scary. How will you handle fear? This is a question that you will have to answer, and sometimes you answer more with your actions than words, as you engage in the process of leaving the familiarity of a job. There are some things you can count on when you work a traditional job, including a regular paycheck, insurance and someone else taking the risks and setting the rules.

In *The Truman Show*, the main character is part of a script, and his life is merely a scripted reality show. Eventually, the main character, played by Jim Carrey, discovers the deception, decides to escape and eventually finds his way to the end zone of the set. He must confront his fear of leaving the fake reality that he has come to know as his life.

DECEPTION

In the child's tale *The Emperor's New Clothes*, the deceived king of the land parades in front of the crowd nude while everyone pretends he has on the best suit of clothes ever, until a little boy has the nerve to call out, "He doesn't have anything on!"

How many of us are afraid to admit that our jobs are ill-suited and we're parading in the nude? How many of us are prepared to admit that working our job requires a slave mentality, and the real fruits of our entrapment are frustration, a false sense of security, minimal wages, and a life-time living on Barely-Getting-By Street? We are faking it, and in reality, we're nude. How sad!

It is said that we are the emperor or ruler of our own lives, but when it comes to our careers, we are walking around naked. Like the lion, the real cage is in our minds, or like the elephant, one of the most powerful beasts in the animal kingdom, we are tied to stakes made by others. It is time for us to break free.

> *"Discontent is the catalyst for change."*
> *- Dr. Mike Murdock*
> *Minister, author and entrepreneur*

CHAPTER 6
The Courageous Truth

"In my lectures, I frequently ask how many people do not like what they do to earn money. Some people find their jobs tolerable, but the vast majority do not like what they do to make a living. Most people have a job for which they're paid just enough not to quit, and they work just hard enough not to get fired. Only a very few really love the work they do.... We have unwittingly associated the process of making money with something that's painful or, at best, not pleasurable."

- Russ Whitney
Author of <u>Building Wealth</u>

To begin our journey of finding a job more suited to who we are, a job that is tailor-made for us, first we need to face the truth. Simply put, are we unhappy in the job we are working now? There can be a myriad of reasons that the cloud of discontent is hovering over the method you've chosen to make a living.

What is your career GPS telling you? Do any of the following statements ring true?

- I don't like my job.
- I hate Mondays.

- I'll never get the promotion or the money I feel I deserve here.
- I'm playing someone else's game on their turf...this is not where I belong.
- I dislike my boss.
- I dislike the office politics.
- I've bought into a generational belief that doesn't fit me anymore: The way to success is to work hard. Whether or not you like what you're doing is not as important as placing your ladder on the wall, in the career arena, even if it's the wrong wall.
- My job actually makes me want to cry, and I don't see a way out.
- My job makes me physically sick. I feel my stomach turning and my blood pressure raising when I am in the workplace.
- My skills and abilities are not appreciated by my boss or co-workers.
- It is time to pursue work that is better suited to my interests, talents and skills.
- At one season, this was the right job, but I have changed and my interests have changed. The job I chose to do at 20 is not a good fit for who I have become at 45.
- I'd rather be an entrepreneur than work a traditional job.
- I'm free-spirited and self-directed. A traditional job just doesn't fit my personality.

Which statements best fit you? If the reasons you want to change jobs is different from the above, take time to write them down. What's your motivation? Why do you feel the need to change your current job or pursue making a living in a different field? It's important to know your "why". Acknowledging why the job doesn't suit you is key in helping you find work you enjoy.

Did you initially choose the wrong field or settle for your job because it was the best offer you had at the time? Maybe when you decided to join your company, making money outweighed finding a suitable career. Perhaps your passions and interests have changed since you made your career choice or maybe the work culture and company's mission have changed. But now, your gut keeps screaming, "IT'S TIME FOR A CHANGE!" Finally, you are prepared to listen.

You know it's time to correct your course and steer your career-ship in another direction.

> *"We've been taught for generations to play it safe; you get a job and don't make waves. I contend that's the most dangerous thing that you can possibly do.*
> *- Douglas Kriger*
> *Professional speaker*

Chapter 7
Clock-Watchers

"Proverbs 18:16 is a powerful statement... 'A man's gift makes room for him.' ...You were designed to be known for your gift. God has put a gift or talent into every person that the world will make room for. It is this gift that will enable you to fulfill your vision. It will make a way for you in life. It is in exercising this gift that you will find real fulfillment, purpose, and contentment in your work."
- Dr. Myles Monroe
<u>*The Principles and Power of Vision*</u>

There is something inside that's restless and knows it's time for a career change. It's the actions and voices inside that we sometimes refuse to pay attention to, because it's a call to action. When you're not working your dream job, when your work no longer feeds your soul, you feel and know it, even when you try to ignore the soul's unrest. Subconsciously, you know that it's not the job that makes your gifts and passion shine. Worst yet, the job drains your energy, and it's hard to go there each day without anxiously waiting for the day to end. Like a bad pair of shoes you can hardly wait to remove, you've turned into this work-beast called the clock-watcher.

You anxiously wait for 5:00 pm to come. You start packing 15 minutes before 5. The last hour before quitting time moves dreadfully slow, the last minutes even slower. Have you taken the time to ask yourself why?

Perhaps you know the job is not what you were called, anointed or born to do. In your gut, you know you are in the wrong field. Maybe during a certain season, the job suited who you were, but not now. The career decision you made at 18 or 22 is different than the one you would make today.

Maybe, *they* would not have approved of your decision. Who are the *theys*? Whoever they are, they don't have to sign in for you at 8 am each morning after making that dreadful commute to work in grid-lock traffic. Whether parents, teachers, friends or neighbors, how long are you going to give your power of decision-making over to the *theys*? Own your life. Get out of the cage of others' opinions or what you suppose their opinion would be. Stop giving your power over to the *theys* and what you imagine they will think.

When you feel an underlying restlessness and boredom, and you have officially become a clock-watcher, it's time to make a career change.

Dave Ramsey, a financial guru who urges his followers to get and stay out of debt, recently commented on his talk show about the impact the coronavirus has had on our lives. While sad, he said, it's not all bad. According to Ramsey, 70 percent of the people in the United States do not like their job, and as many as 80 percent worldwide are dissatisfied with their jobs. Ramsey tells his listeners that the pandemic makes people see the ramifications of staying in debt and not building a financial safety net. Furthermore, the coronavirus, as unfortunate as the event has been, should make people think about the ways in which they earn their money.

When your work is connected to your calling and you are doing what you enjoy, you tend not to be a clock-watcher. You're not frustrated and bored. Some people actually enjoy what they're doing, and the time rushes by.

> *"When making money becomes your hobby, getting up early is no longer a chore. Staying late doesn't matter, because you're enjoying yourself. In fact, you'll be having so much fun that you'll toss out the time clock. You won't need it. And when you find the right vehicle that lets making money become your hobby, you'll find yourself generating significantly more dollars in much less time than you're spending on your job right now."*
> *- Russ Whitney*
> *Entrepreneur and author of Building Wealth*

CHAPTER 8
The Jobless Quest

"No matter what challenge you may be facing, you must remember that while the canvas of your life is painted with daily experiences, behaviors, reactions, and emotions, you're the one controlling the brush. If I had known this at 21, I could have saved myself a lot of heartache and self-doubt. It would have been a revelation to understand that we are all the artists of our own lives—and that we can use as many colors and brushstrokes as we like."
- Oprah Winfrey
Media entrepreneur, television producer, talk-show host, actress and philanthropist

JOURNAL

After acknowledging your inner calling towards joblessness, next it's important to devise a plan. How will you move towards your inner longing to change careers or embrace entrepreneurship?

Start a jobless journal or get out a sheet of paper (for now) and write 20 or 30 reasons you are personally drawn towards joblessness. What makes you want to pursue money-making opportunities that naturally align with your gifts, talents and skills? As a popular quote attributed to many, including Confucius and Marc Anthony, says, "Choose a job you love, and you will never have to work a day in your life."

Journaling is a great tool for identifying your gifts, examining your motivations and navigating your path. Know your whys. Why is it important to pursue a career you love? Keep the reasons before you in your special jobless journal. Identify your motives: why do you want a different career? A key component in persevering in challenging times is remembering your driving force.

"When you change your mind, you change your life." This phrase has been well-used for decades. Take time to fill your journal with not only your insights and plans, but even your fears. Examine any thoughts that are barriers to making necessary moves. In examining these thoughts, let your strong, confident, fearless self step forth and make a rebuttal to the underlying negativity. A jobless journal can be a valuable tool for dissecting objectionable thoughts as you redirect your focus on enjoyable income-producing activities. The journal gives you a place to hear and talk to yourself about the changes you want to make. And, yes, you will have to make changes.

Talking to yourself is not weird; you talk to yourself unconsciously, hundreds (or perhaps thousands) of times each day. So why not turn your inner conversations into fuel? There are some questions that only you can answer for yourself. It is time to move towards joblessness so it can take form instead of just hanging in that void, shapeless zone.

Joan, a mother of four, realized her work schedule made it almost impossible to spend the needed time to parent her children. This became her motivation for changing careers. She wanted to go on field trips in the middle of the day, to pick her children up from school and to be home when the kids arrived home from school each day and whenever they were sick. Her need to parent took precedence over her career. She began to journal to help her carve out a path to her goals. It gave her an place to listen to her inner GPS, and it helped her stay focused on her dreams.

QUESTIONING YOURSELF

Questions are important. The following are some questions you can consider as you prepare for a career change:

- What will you do on the other side of 9 to 5, when you are no longer at your present job?
- What makes you feel alive? What lights your inner spark?
- What makes you freeze on the threshold of making a career change?
- Do you have an emergency fund to help successfully take on this challenge, or do you need to build an emergency fund?
- Rather than an emergency fund, maybe you need to build an opportunity fund. How will you go about doing so? Will you have $50 deducted from your paycheck every two weeks so you'll have money to pursue your goals? What specific plan can you implement?
- Do you need to pay off a loan, pay off credit cards or stop using your plastic money so you can build a stronger financial foundation?
- Is your real goal becoming an entrepreneur? If so, what services or products do you see yourself providing? What training will you need?
- What do you need to do to prepare for the least turbulent road in a career change?
- Who around you can mentor or encourage you as you seek to make the move?

- Are you plagued by fear or lack of confidence when it comes to doing what you love and turning it into a money-making venture?
- What if you fail the first time or second time out? Are you ready to stick to your goals of finding your way to joblessness?

Now include your uniquely designed questions as you examine your "whys" for moving towards joblessness. Commitment is key. A designated place to write (your writing journal), a designated time to write (the first ten minutes of your lunch break) and even doing a jobless vision board will signal to your soul and consciousness how determined you are to create a healthy income that is not dependent on you punching a time-clock.

So, ride the waves of self-examination and move along your pathway to jobless independence with style and in a way that honors you, your thirst and your quest. Use your jobless journal to explore and map out possible courses of action. Use your journal to research or brainstorm. Draw, cut-and-paste and color to make your journal uniquely your own.

"Have a belief in yourself that is bigger than anyone's disbelief."

- August Wilson
Playwright and winner of two Pulitzer Prizes for Drama

CHAPTER 9

Transformation

"People crave change. But they are afraid of leaving the familiar behind. They want to do something different, but they don't know how different they want it to be. So, they stay where they are. And day after day, they feel more and more boxed in by life."
- *Marti Smye*
Consultant, speaker and author of books including <u>Is It Too Late to Run Away and Join the Circus?</u>

When my sister, Pauline Lampkin, lost her job in the banking industry, after dealing with the immediate issues unemployment brings, and after much deliberation, she decided to change careers. She returned to school, received a master's degree and credentials to become an educator, which offered her more financial security and suited her personal goals better. The hours were not as long, and she was off in the summers and could spend more time with her husband and three children.

Pauline not only enjoyed being a high school science teacher, but she was better compensated in her new position.

My friend, Darnell Sandifer, refers to himself as free-spirited. He says, "It's a trap. You could be a good citizen and do what they tell you to do and you're still just going to be mediocre."

Although for some years Darnell worked a traditional job, he readily admits, "I never enjoyed people telling me what to do."

Since a child, he said he's known that the traditional job place was not his calling. "Do what you have to do until something comes your way or falls into your lap."

Darnell worked for the railroad and in the computer and banking industry before eventually finding himself unemployed. He decided to change directions and begin investing time and money into real estate and becoming an entrepreneur. Darnell and his wife, Odette, have become financially free and are able to travel; furthermore, for Darnell, controlling his time and setting his own schedule is a wonderful gift.

For both Darnell and Pauline, making changes required some soul-searching moments, faith and courage.

THE COCOON

The struggle helps the caterpillar transform into a butterfly. The new butterfly, in all its splendor, doesn't emerge from the cocoon without the struggle—the struggle is necessary.

We try to avoid the struggle. We equate the struggle with problems, pain, difficulties and all the terms that can send a shiver through our spine. But unfortunately (or fortunately), the struggle is part of the yellow brick road as we make our way to a place of success.

The wicked witches, the challenges and the obstacles all help create the sweetness of the success we seek.

At the end of perseverance—despite the difficulty, the resilience after the fall, the patience during the wait, the self-discipline and prayer as you face the troll who blocks the bridge leading to achievement—is the manifestation of the dreams, goals and visions you've carried in the wombs of your spirit and heart.

I think it's important to teach children about change and transformation. Two family publishing projects both tackle the subject of change: *Silly Caterpillar* and *Today My Sister Is Getting Married.*

There are two lessons I hope children walk away with after reading these books. In *Silly Caterpillar,* change doesn't always feel comfortable, but still it's necessary. In order for the caterpillar to become the butterfly he's destined to be, he has to tune out his *bug* critics and go into the darkness of his cocoon for a period of time for the transformation to take place.

In *Today My Sister is Getting Married*, the flower girl, who is grieving the fact that her older sister is moving out of the house, has to put her love for her sister above her own feelings, because even though she'll miss her sister, the flower girl wants her sister happy.

As adults, we sometimes forget that even when change seems scary, when change is unwanted, when we have to push ourselves toward the change, changing and transitions are not necessarily bad. Are you willing to pay attention to the silent scream inside saying it's time for a change? Are you willing to resist fear? If so, consider the following.

- Changing careers or moving into entrepreneurship requires courage. If your courage muscles are under-developed, it's not too late; they can be developed. Change your self-talk, and tell yourself why you deserve to work in a way that's more suited to you, a way that honors who you are and your unique God-given gifts.

- After writing your reasons for wanting to make a career change in your journal, reread them. On rough days, your reasons can keep you afloat.
- Continue to tell yourself you deserve to work in a way most suitable to you; tell yourself this is possible.
- Read books, watch documentaries or find real-life mentors who are living their best lives and are making money in ways that honor their talents and passions.
- Begin examining obstacles that might hinder the pursuit of your just-right career. Is it that car note that you wish you had never signed for? Are you addicted to using credit cards?
- Take actions that will support your quest for joblessness. Enroll in school, but be mindful of not accumulating school loans. Start a savings account to help support you as you change careers or fund your education or begin your entrepreneur endeavors.
- Begin by researching money-making ventures or businesses that spark your interest. Keep track of what you find in your jobless journal.
- Did you start your journal? Do you have a written plan? If not, start one today. It doesn't have to be perfect, and you can alter it as you gain momentum and knowledge. Determine that you will stick to your plan. Even when joblessness becomes the cry of your soul, making the required changes will require patience, diligence and planning. Keep working your plan.
- Celebrate little wins. If you feel changing direction could take longer than you would want, persevere; it's important to stay with your plan. Changing directions could mean being willing to get training in the area of your interest, paying off debt, building a client-base for your new business, or

gradually moving in a new direction, but don't quit. Tap into your pool of courage and resourcefulness. Continue implementing changes, whether on a small or large scale, this will help you to obtain and sustain your quest.
- Build your resilience muscles. There may be days when you feel overwhelmed or hopeless. Don't let these days blindside you. Be prepared to deal with the discouragement. Learn to encourage yourself. Watch movies like *Men of Honor,* based on a true story in which Cuba Gooding, who plays a starring role, becomes an amputee after an accident but still refuses to give up his dream of becoming a deep-sea diver. Learn how to keep yourself going in the face of adversity, when the going is slow or when your goals of happy employment seem impossible.
- Add your own list of affirmations to your journal. The day will come when you will want (and need) to read them.

"Fear will always knock at your door. Just don't invite it in for dinner. And for heaven's sake, don't offer it a bed for the night."
- *Max Lucado*
   <u>*Fearless*</u>

CHAPTER 10
God, Take Care of this Goose

"Maybe you harbor the desire to do a certain kind of work that you're not engaged in now. Maybe you have recurring thoughts about something you need to accomplish in your life. This inner voice is not arbitrary. These thoughts aren't just passing through your mind like a breeze. They're tugging at you, shaking you up for a reason. What's going on?
It's your destiny calling.
Truly, this is the very thing you're supposed to be doing in your life."

- Tyler Perry
Actor, film-producer and author of books, including
<u>Higher Is Waiting</u>

DEFERRED DREAMS

Maria put off her dreams and goals for some time in the distant future, often speaking of what she'd do in retirement. Traveling and becoming a full-time artist were at the top of her verbal bucket list. Work and raising her two sons depleted her energy, money and time as she spent year after year going to a job that didn't awake her passion. Surviving the moment was paramount. Real enjoyment was put off until the kids were older and there would be more disposable income. She hardly ever considered her here and now; like the topic of a Langston Hughes poem, her dreams were deferred.

What about adding joy into our lives now? Many are caught in the quicksand of job dissatisfaction, ignoring the loudness of time clicking by. One day the ticking will stop, and you'll have to face your mortality, and your deferred dreams.

Deferring your dreams for a mediocre lifestyle at best can leave you with regrets, especially when you're merely living from paycheck to paycheck. You tell yourself there will be more time and money at retirement. But as retirement approaches, you know your golden years won't be so golden. How do you live on a portion of your income when it was difficult living on it all?

HAPPINESS

There's a sign on my bedroom wall: "Do more of what makes you happy." Some of us put off the trips we want to take, the sculpturing class we'd like to enroll in, learning how to swim, hiring a piano teacher or finding a more satisfactory job, or starting income-producing business activities that would enrich our lives.

You can convince yourself to remain in a holding position for a host of reasons: there's not enough time, there's not enough money or there's more important issues on your plate now, like caring for a love one or paying down credit cards.

But what about doing more of what makes you happy *now*? After all, all you have is now. Be determined to *enjoy everyday life*, as Joyce Meyer often says. Put *you* in your life. You count. Your feelings count. What keeps you attached to a job that doesn't make room for your individual gifts and passions? Have you explored this in your journal? Many say they can't afford to pursue their job or business dreams. Could the real issue be fear? Fear of risks? Fear of change? Fear of leaving the familiar? Go for it. Write down all the reasons, excuses and fears in your journal; get them out of your head and onto the page, where you can see them, confront them and challenge them.

Sadly, after working over two decades in a draining job, my very talented artist friend, Maria, realized her dream of raising two productive young men; however, she succumbed to an illness. Traveling and pursuing her art career remained on her bucket list. Her retirement and 401K went to family.

When I walk past the picture on my living room wall that Maria painted, it reminds me not to bury my gifts. I must trust my talents and unleash my deferred dreams.

One day, reality will visit, and you will realize that everything you needed was always under your control. Only you can take your life in a different direction. You are in charge of your employment decisions. If you are not happy, you have the option of doing something different or doing nothing at all. You can't continually put off your life for a paycheck then for retirement.

COURAGE

It takes courage to admit that the job you have devoted years to is no longer the job you desire. To implement a plan for a career change and then to work and plan your way out of a job means putting on your hero suit.

Situations arise that force you out of a less-than-ideal job, like sickness, cutbacks, the closing of your company, being fired, or worse yet, the coronavirus. Initially you may flounder and reach for any job to keep you afloat.

It will require faith and courage, and determination, not to just settle for *any* job. Sometimes a *triggering event* places you in a mode where you can no longer merely tread the career waters, but you must make needful, yet tough, job decisions.

Joblessness takes courage to handle, whether it's thrust upon you or something you seek. While joblessness can be a weird sort of gift—offering you a chance to be free to explore your environment, community and analyze your life—it can require tremendous fortitude to navigate through unfamiliar waters and to find peaceful financial and work-satisfactory shores. Without taking action or forward motion, sometimes like my friend Maria, you resign yourself to living an unfulfilling workplace life.

FREEDOM

In the movie *Amistad*, directed by Steven Spielberg, actor Djimon Hounsou playing Joseph Clinque, an enslaved African, shouts, "Give us, us free!" Perhaps freedom is a burning desire of your soul. The real *work* is continuing in a job that no longer ignites your passion, while the cries for freedom strongly radiate within your soul.

The desire will become like kindling to a fire, so strong that you too will refuse to wait for the freedom your heart longs for. "Give us, us free!" You are finally emotionally aligned to pay the cost for the freedom you seek; the price it will take to become independently employed or change careers.

THE GOOSE

Change often brings the need for self-sacrificing and the application of courage. Even as slaves bought their own freedom, the desire to be free has to be so strong within you that you have no choice but to make the necessary sacrifices.

At one point, the price for me was to forgo my health insurance or figure out a way to include the insurance in an already stretched budget. After much consideration, I found a way to send the $417.99 into the board of education for my medical and dental insurance, while my head voice said, "You can't afford that, and even though you paid for your insurance this month, you won't be able to pay it again next month."

While one voice discouraged me, my positive inner voice simply said, "Have faith." Most of the things I have accomplished in my life required faith. I believe that somehow God provides the finances, the encouragement, the strength, the wisdom, or whatever I need.

In that season of my life, I felt I needed and deserved health insurance. After all, I was the goose who had laid the golden eggs. The goose who had raised three children, maintained a household in a sought-after community and returned to school as a single parent to get my master's degree.

I was the goose who needed annual mammograms, who need dental and eye care, the goose who wanted to go to my primary care doctor. I was the goose who needed her hair done, her yearly medical checkup, electricity, telephone, and mortgage payments. Finally, the positive head-voice won out. I embraced my courage and affirmed," If God sees after the sparrow, surely He'd see after this goose."

THE COSTS

Staying in my current job was no longer an option. There are underlying prices you pay for an unsuitable job, and I wasn't willing to pay them. Mind you, it's not that the job itself, as an educator, was bad. For some, it would have been their ideal job, but for me, destiny was calling me to change paths.

The cost of staying when it's time for you to move could be losing your authentic self; your happiness quota suffers and the quality of your daily life declines. I wasn't willing to face never connecting to my true purpose and living a life plagued by fears and regrets.

> *"Too many people pass away with their songs unsung, their gifts unwrapped, their talents unused, and their treasures left buried."*
> *- Vickie Daniel*
> *Vocalist and record company owner*

Chapter 11
No Regrets

"Do what you love; you'll be better at it. It sounds pretty simple, but you'd be surprised how many people don't get this one right away."
- LL Cool J
Record producer, actor and entrepreneur

FREEDOM

For Harriet Tubman, the time had come; she knew she would rather die than live life as a slave. Harriet Tubman decided to run away, to head north. In spite of her challenges—feeling lost, fearful, hungry and being pursued—with God's help and with the help of the Underground Railroad, Harriet found her way to freedom.

Freedom tasted as good as she supposed. The runaway slave, with a bounty on her back, tossed the possibility of death and danger aside, only to return to the South again and again to help bring others to freedom. Harriet hated slavery. For her, slavery had become intolerable.

When you make a decision that you only have one life and you will spend it doing what you love, catering to the essence of who you are, the confines of traditional employment become intolerable.

Everyone will not thirst for the freedom you seek, the desire to be free from the drudgery of a 9 to 5, the freedom to work in rewarding ways, freedom to employ your unique gifts and talents. Refuse to let your *new job* become convincing them.

Well-beaten paths are sometimes paths of comfort. Everyone is not willing to take the risk and leave well-beaten paths. Traveling alone through the darkness to an unfamiliar place means facing uncertainty, but be brave. Muster up your Harriet Tubman spirit.

TRUST YOURSELF

Self-doubt, fear and indecision can become barriers preventing you from moving in the direction of recapturing your dreams; you may also be required to learn new skills. If you're feeling overwhelmed, practice controlling your negative feelings with inner rebuttals. Affirm: I was put on this earth for better things, not to financially and emotionally live on "This-will-have-to-do Street." Begin allocating space in your journal for positive affirmations to counter negativity.

Even under the shadow of inner protesting, "I can't afford to take off from my job to get the training I need, or I can't afford tuition," begin your journey. Your job is to bridge the gap between your ideal job or business, or whatever you've decide to do within the bounds of legality and morality, to make money.

If you're lacking in skills and experience, volunteer; work for an organization in the field of your interest. Think of this as an apprenticeship. "I don't have time to give my services away for free," you may protest, but look at this as an opportunity to gain the knowledge you need, while investing in yourself. Volunteering today prepares you for compensation in a field you love tomorrow. Furthermore, your payment will exceed experience; while "working free," you'll benefit in the currency of personal satisfaction and relationship building, which could lead to future income-producing opportunities.

If education seems to be the greatest barrier between you and your soul's calling, get creative. The world has changed. It is more possible today than it was in the past to pursue the knowledge you need for a career change, in a low-residency school program or by taking on-line classes. Many colleges and educational facilities now offer students an opportunity for training with few or no requirements for physically being present on the school grounds. It is easier now, than ever before, to pursue a degree or training in an area that could usher you into a new job direction, in a way tailored to your individual needs, without financially draining you.

You are the catalyst for mustering up the confidence needed to overcome the roadblocks between you and your desirable career. In her book *Steppin' Out with Attitude,* Anita Bunkley says, "If you decide to drastically change your current situation, be brave, be patient, be honest. Don't allow fear of losing what has become familiar to prevent you from developing your potential or fulfilling what you consider your destiny."

Adopt an attitude that works for you and not against you as you move towards a pleasurable career. Don't let excuses sentence you to the sidelines, separating you from your dream-work.

THE POWER OF SMALL CHANGES

Marva Collins, a renowned educator, was once asked, "How do you eat an elephant?" She responded, "One bite at the time."

First, you set a goal of eating the elephant. Next, you take the first bite. Let your reason for leaving the job become bigger than the challenges you will face. Not wanting to die a bitter old lady in a rocking chair, mumbling about the dances I never had, the songs I never sung, the places I never got the courage to visit or what I could have been or done, has been motivation enough for me to take my first bite of adventure.

The scriptures tell us not to despise small beginnings; self-help gurus invite us to swiss-cheese our way to success. We cannot discount changes even when they are small.

THERE'S POWER IN SILENCE

There have been times when it was necessary to hide a child who was destined for kingship. Joseph was thrown in the pit because he had a dream. Moses was put in a basket because the enemies were searching for him to kill him because he was a child with a destiny.

Sometimes it is necessary to keep silent and not to share our dreams with dream killers, those who wouldn't understand, those who are so anchored in *systematic thinking* and feel their duty is to save you from yourself and the harm you're going to encounter pursuing your dreams.

Sometimes the best thing you can do while planning your escape from the mundaneness of your job, is just to say nothing.

As much as you might feel compelled to share your plans of leaving your current job with coworkers, friends or family, it might not be the time. When you decide to share your dreams, make sure you are selective about who to share them with. It's important to distinguish between dream-killers and dream-builders. Usually those who resist pursuing their own soul callings, may be insensitive and unwilling to help you read your road map to freedom. They may not even understand your inclination to change careers. Sharing your goals with people who don't understand your dream of becoming meaningfully employed, could become a hindrance and distraction, and only delay you. You don't want to add their paralyzing fears, thoughts and opinions about your move as you grapple with own.

In her book, *Making a Living Without a Job,* Barbara J. Winters states the following. "Far too often, the people who block our goals are those whom we expected to support and encourage us.

But change, which can be frightening, may be even more fearful to the ones around you. If you change direction, if you go after your dreams, if you succeed, will you still love them? If your life becomes what you want it to be, will theirs look even more drab by comparison? Keep in mind that people who block you are saying more about themselves than they are about you."

When you expect others, even those who are close to you, to understand your motivation for wanting to change career directions, you set yourself up for disappointment.

Keep in mind, it's not that people are intentionally being mean, your vision is unique to you and was given to you; they have not been given your goals, insights and desires. Somethings are better left unexplained until experience, time, and growth can give voice to the explanation. So preserve your energy for focusing on your pursuit of change. Shhhhhhhhhh. Practice the art of silence. You don't need others' approval.

NO REGRETS

In his book *Life Lessons*, Robert C. Savage offers this advice, "Live each day as if it's your last—it may be."

My sister and I often remind each other that this is no dress rehearsal! We must make a conscious effort to enjoy life and to live it consciously.

What if you change jobs and don't really like your new position? Is it better to have made the change or to have remained in your present position?

Life will end for us all, and when we face its ending, we don't want to have regrets. People say they regret the things they didn't try, not the things they did try. Give yourself freedom to try and face failure. Don't let *the fear of failure* defeat you.

"If you want to create the life of your dreams, then you are going to have to take 100% responsibility for your life.... This means giving up all your excuses, all your victim stories, all the reasons why you can't and why you haven't up until now, and all your blaming of outside circumstances. You have to give them all up forever."
- Jack Canfield
Speaker and author of several books including <u>The Success Principles</u>

Chapter 12

Sixteen Tons: Feeling Deserving

"We spend a lot of time doing things we don't want to do in places we don't want to be, for no other reason than we feel we have to. We have to bring home a paycheck, please our friends and family, and meet the expectations the world has set for us. If nothing else, we find ourselves in less than ideal situations out of habit. We follow the path our lives begin to take and are too afraid or reluctant to change our course as time goes by."
- Richard Chang
Author of <u>The Passion Plan</u>

Remember Tennessee Ernie Ford's song? "You load sixteen tons, what do you get? Another day older and deeper in debt. Saint Peter, don't you call me 'cause I can't go...I owe my soul to the company store." Or Donna Summer's song, "She works hard for the money. So hard for it honey." Debt often lingers on your doorstep. Lyrics, posters and other mementos often remind us that for many, work and pleasure don't live in the same neighborhood. Many may see work as a necessity, not necessarily something to be enjoyed.

In a recent Harvard Business Review article, Susan Peppercorn states that 85 percent of employees aren't engaged in their jobs, according to Gallup statistics. Peppercorn also says,

"Given that the average person spends 90,000 hours at work in a lifetime, it's important to figure out how to feel better about the time you spend earning a living."

How many succumb to spending decades in jobs they don't enjoy? Looking for employment where your skill sets, your interests and talents can all be honored is challenging; however, staying in an unsuitable job is much worse.

By now, your personal jobless journal has started to come alive and is taking on its unique shape; it is providing the needed wisdom and information. If you have decided to climb out of the traditional work barrel, refusing to accept joyless work, another step in the process will be finding others who believe that pleasure and productivity doesn't have to be at odds. Align yourself with people and communities who support pleasurable work. Find your tribe—people and organizations that celebrate pleasurable work.

GUARD YOUR MOUTH

Your mouth can work for you or against you as you search for meaningful work. When seeking to bring passion into your work, even when it seems like an insurmountable task, it's important to watch your words. Changing what you say can help change your beliefs and free you from a prison of negativity. You must avoid words that arise from the souls of the hopeless.

- "Work is work and you don't have to like it, as long as it gives you a paycheck."
- "What makes you think you have to enjoy work? Enjoy your weekends."
- "Your mom has been at her job for 25 years. Do you think she likes it?"

- "What makes you think jobs are to be enjoyed?"
- "Whether you like it or not is not the point. It's a good job, and it pays you well. *Like* the paycheck."
- "A job that you like? Who cares if you like it or not? Sounds like you're just a little lazy to me."
- "Stop complaining. After all, it helps make ends meet. It could be a lot worst. At least you have a job."
- "No one enjoys their job."

With statements like the above, you're defeated before you even start your search. You have to be determined not to let the negative opinions and beliefs of others prevent you from crossing the bridge to work that is both emotionally and financially rewarding. Statements full of negativity won't be heard in the conversations of your new tribe; still, it will be important to learn to affirm and support yourself. (This will be discussed in Chapter 23.) Meaningful and profitable work is not merely an illusion. For some, however, it could mean becoming an entrepreneur.

CHOOSING TO CREATE OUR WORK

As I watch the owner of a chain of local fast food restaurants make his regular rounds to his eating establishments, I am reminded that work and fun can walk peacefully beside one another. As he moves slowly through the entrance and the sun highlights his silver-gray hair, I think, *he'll never spend all the money he's already made.*

His many employees get out of the way to let him do what he appears to enjoy, being hands-on. He grabs a white apron then some potatoes and begins to peel them and chop them for fresh homemade

French fries, an item the hamburger place is known for. It appears passion is his driving force.

I assume he visits his restaurants not merely as an act of accountability, but because wants to. Obviously, he enjoys what he does, and his payoff exceeds merely monetary compensation, but an aurora of personal satisfaction and contentment seems to feel his face.

Becoming an entrepreneur is not the solution for everyone. It could mean spending more time working rather than considerably less time. It is, however, a choice uniquely your own. For some, self-employment brings financial rewards and autonomy beyond their dreams. For others, business ownership means trusting your ability to be self-directed and take risks, so it only leads to frustration and anxiety.

In her book *How to Be an Entrepreneur and Keep Your Sanity,* Paula McCoy Pinderhuges asks, "Where would you rather be at 6:00 am in the morning? In the shower getting ready to go work for someone else's dream or in your pajamas, laptop in hand, putting the final touches on your own?" The choice belongs to you. When self-employment became an option for me, I decided to try it; so, I traded in long commutes and job security for entrepreneurship.

THE PLUNGE

When I decided to take the plunge and become independently employed, it surprised me that a significant number of people approached me to "secretly" say that was their dream too: to get off the grindstone, to work for themselves, to get out of the rat race, to kiss their job goodbye.

What surprised me even more were the people perched by the pool of joblessness but afraid to jump in.

My friend Gloria gave me excuse after excuse for continuing to work a job she had grown weary of. *"I have too much debt. It's Christmas time (she continued to pull that plastic out and spend). I don't have enough years.* I asked her now many years she had. *"Only 20,"* was the reply. I looked at her questioningly. She added, *"I would have to pay my own health insurance."* Yet, she and her husband had several personal living residences. Gloria died two months after she retired.

There will always be reasons not to, but can you find a reason to leap? What good will it do to spend another year at a job to add a 5 percent increase to your retirement if some unforeseen event like sickness or premature death forces you out of the workplace and you never get a chance to enjoy the fruits of retirement? Even when the retirement fruits are hanging low, some are apprehensive about reaching for them.

OVERCOMING SELF-DOUBT

It's sad to think that in recent years, payday stores have risen up in our communities to make profit from the fact that after giving our hours, days and years to a less than satisfactory job, many of us can't even make it from payday to payday.

If you keep doing what you've done in the past, you can't expect a lot to be different in the future. Implementing some of the suggestions in this book—keeping a jobless journal, monitoring your self-talk, finding mentors—will put you on your own cheer-leading team and in the direction of being joyfully employed. Small actions can go a long way in helping you reach your goals of meaningful work. Be creative and determined. Learning to encourage yourself is a lighthouse, guiding you to the shores of safety and joblessness. Working should be seen as a contribution to mankind, a way of being productive, a means of getting compensated for your strengths, gifts and talents, not a life sentence.

By deciding to strengthen your courage muscles and move in your uniquely designed employment direction, you are voting for yourself. You have become an ally, rather than a foe, to obtaining your personal work goals. Burn the mental ships that tell you work can't be pleasurable. Decide that regardless of how long it takes, you can no longer work year after year in a job you don't love, merely for the sake of racking up those weekly, monthly or bi-weekly paychecks.

Continue to build up your desire and courage, and strengthen your resolve to trim back excessive spending as you pursue your goal of becoming happily jobless, a dream that has become more real to you than ever before.

You are far from settling for that 16-tons-and- what-do-you-get lifestyle. The vision is clear; with your courage and faith muscles, you are committed to moving forth.

Journaling and paying attention have taught you lessons that you can use now or later in your pursuit. What about risks? What about fears? These are feelings you will have to continually confront.

What if I make a mistake? Making mistakes as you explore the world of entrepreneurship, change careers, and seek income through your passions is bound to happen. However, failure is a classroom, not a permanent state. Sometimes failing becomes part of the costs in finally succeeding. Failure is part of the price you must be willing to pay as you muster up the courage and make the brave decision to go in a different direction.

When we take on the adventure of exploring a new world or a new way of living, when we get lost, when we make a wrong turn, fail or make mistakes, remember *U-turns* are permissible.

"Remind yourself regularly that you are better than you think you are.... Successful people are just ordinary folks who have developed belief in themselves and what they do. Never—yes, never—sell yourself short."
- Dr. David J. Schwartz
Author of The Magic of Thinking Big

CHAPTER 13

Write the Vision

*"You've heard the saying 'TGIF. Thank God it's Friday.'
For you and me it also should be, 'TGIM. Thank God it's
Monday.'
'TGIW. Thank God it's Wednesday.'
'TDIS. Thank God it's Sunday.'"*

*- Joel Osteen
Minister and author of books including <u>Every Day a
Friday: How to Be Happier 7 Days a Week</u>*

LEAVING BOARD OF EDUCATION PROSPEROUSLY (LBOEP)

I taught school for many years. It was a good job, and it gave to me, and I gave to it. It helped me raise my three children as a single parent. But as Ecclesiastes says, "To everything there is a season," and my season and mindset had changed. I was not longer willing to get up at six each morning and go to a job that I had begun to think of as limiting. I reasoned with myself: *I can only have a 20-minute lunch break; it could be high stress, especially after years of getting children who had behavioral problems and the expectations of the educational board was sometimes like being on a roller coaster.* Dealing with troubled youth, disrespect from students and classroom discipline became more and more of a challenge. At one point, I could feel my blood pressure rise in the middle of teaching a reading lesson. Emotionally and physically, I was getting the message that my time of working with the board of education was coming to an end. I realized that for some, teaching was an ideal job, like it had been for me at one point; but I knew my personal season had changed. Still, I will be forever grateful for having an opportunity to teach, and for the lessons I learned from my co-workers, the students, parents and my position. I started teaching in my early twenties, but the time for change had arrived, and I was growing increasingly discontent. I was suffering from job burn-out.

My awareness that written goals are more powerful than just goals we carry around in our head prompted me to construct a vision sheet that merely said: LBOEP: *leave the board of education prosperously.* Thus, I began my journey. I was able to take several sabbaticals with no pay. I survived. I was able to cut back on my credit card spending. I learned to drive my car for a few years longer, thereby eliminating a car note. I was able to redirect some of my paycheck towards a growing real estate portfolio. I was able to bypass designer bags, shoes, and add more to my 401K or 403B—another way of saving money I would need for my transition.

Finally, the day came when the board offered a plan that I didn't quite fit into, but I was bold enough to ask if I could take advantage of the early retirement plan. It was called the five plus five. You could add five years of service or five years of age to qualify to leave. I applied, even though my situation didn't quite fit the cookie-cutter and needed to be considered on a unique basis. I got the *yes* I needed to move me further down the road of LBOEP. Still, other problems began to surface. How would I buy back time I had lost by taking money from my retirement account decades earlier? I needed credit for the years of service I had forfeited by taking money from my board-managed retirement funds to fill in the many financial gaps. The amount seemed humongous with principal and years of interest added.

Thank God for the wisdom I had used to put money in my 401K and 403B, which I was able to transfer and redirect toward paying several invoices, which came to thousands of dollars needed to continue to pursue my goal of becoming jobless.

Again, jobless doesn't mean workless; I was diligent, but I began working in a different way. I helped manage the real estate I had accumulated to provide a passive income as I struggled to provide as a single parent and to continue pursuing my creative endeavors when I took unpaid sabbaticals.

Today, I am blissfully jobless. I have control over my time, my hours, and my days. If needed, I can take days off for personal field trips, I can travel, work in my pajamas or have an extended lunch with friends or business associations in the middle of the day. I forget at times that I am still working on some level, because my jobs leave me the room for flexibility and for being who I was created to be. I'm able to uniquely design my work to take into consideration who I am, my purpose and my calling. I have a sense of freedom and autonomy. I am grateful.

There is a scripture that says, "Write the vision and make it plain..." (Habakkuk 2:2 KJV).

After writing my vision on an 8.5 by 11 sheet of paper and putting the *LBOEP prosperously* (which meant leave the Board of Education prosperously), I found a stylish, prosperously looking woman wearing an over-sized hat to use as an image on my targeted vision board. I posted the sheet where I could see it. Whereas I knew it was time for a change, I also knew I wasn't willing to live in a season of scarcity I had seen too often in my life.

In the self-help community, experts emphasize the value of written goals and vision boards, stressing the importance of creating them both. If you don't have written career goals, schedule time to write them in your journal. If you already have added your career goals to your journal, schedule a regular time to read them or copy them and hang them up so YOU can see them.

Now is the time to cut pictures from magazines, draw your own pictures or use computerized pictures, but include a visual portrayal of yourself after you've obtained your goal of doing work you love.

If you elect to use a large board for your portrayal, still minimize it and staple a copy into your journal too. Place your vision board and the copies in discreet places, where you can see them often, but out of the way of the scrutiny of others.

My small visual depiction did wonders for me when I needed a boast to remind me that I wanted to live an independently employed but prosperous life. I'm sure yours will inspire you too.

> *"A poll conducted by the Wall Street Journal and ABC News revealed that 50% of Americans would pursue a different profession given the opportunity. I marvel at the phrase, 'given the opportunity.' What opportunity is it we are waiting for? I believe many of us have no clue where to begin, what to look for. We wouldn't recognize the opportunity if it bit us on the nose. The reason remains we are out of touch with our hearts. We simply do not know what it is we would most like to be doing."*
> *- Richard Chang*
> *Author of <u>The Passion Plan</u>*

CHAPTER 14

Getting Out of a Job Rut

> *"If I can go from living out of my car to being on television, there's no telling what God has in store for you. Your life should be more than living from paycheck-to-paycheck and then hoping to collect a pension down the road."*
>
> - Steve Harvey
> Comedian, actor, entrepreneur author of several books including <u>Jump</u>

If a steady paycheck is what inspires you to get up early in the morning and head to work, and if you feel like you are serving a prison sentence instead of contributing to your soul's work or society, then you are probably in a job rut.

Sometimes the tow truck to free you from the trench comes in the form of a life challenge, sickness, a divorce or the death of a family member, friend or other significant other. For some, getting unstuck comes as a company downsizing or not getting the anticipated promotion or worse yet, being fired. For others, getting out of the rut comes as a middle-age crisis or finally mustering up the courage to listen to that wee inner voice warning you you're off course and it's time to change direction. For others, it's just an epiphany: you wake up one morning and say, *I just can't do this for the rest of my life.*

While some settle for a steady paycheck and the security of a job, others ask, "Is this all there is?" Your dreaming and desire muscles awaken; you want to develop your God-given talent; you feel a sense of longing. There's an inner-voice reassuring you that you *can* work in the area of your interest and strengths and make a lucrative income too.

Yes, one voice insists, *"You can do it,"* but then another voice—that inner voice of doubt— is asking, *"Can you really?"* It's like a cartoon: you're walking around with a devil on one shoulder telling you something negative, while the angel on the other shoulder is whispering good things into your ear. You're torn between two worlds and two decisions. Of course, the final vote is yours; you can choose which angel to listen to and what direction to take.

When thoughts fill your head, and there seems to be a devil and an angel fighting, you can choose which one to silence; you're in charge of the remote control.

At moments, you envision yourself sought after for the skills, knowledge and gifts you possess. Then there are times when you envision yourself sick (without insurance), jobless and homeless, begging for rent money and for your next meal.

Convince yourself that you are capable. You can redesign your working life, become your own cheerleader and turn a deaf ear to self-doubt. Switch your inner-radio to a station that is peaceful, powerful, encouraging and supportive as you change your income-producing path.

That cautionary, inner-voice might be asking, what if you fail? However, have you considered what would happen if you succeed? How will succeeding change your life? Even if you fail, you have to give yourself an opportunity to try and to learn from trying, which is called experience.

Recently, I heard Tyler Perry say he had failed enough to pay for a Harvard education 50 times. However, in this season of his life, the world has taken notice because Tyler recently opened a 330-acre entertainment conglomerate with 12 sound stages. The Tyler Perry Studios is the largest film production studio in the United States, and it is said to be larger than even Time Warner.

Tell yourself it's okay to fail, but not allowing yourself to try is not permissible. Try smart, so that you are not paying 50 times for your Harvard education. Get off the sidelines into the arena. Employ an I-know-I-can-do-it spirit, even if changing careers seems far-fetched.

When asked who was his role model, Tyler Perry quickly replied Oprah Winfrey and went on to say that was before he even knew her. You don't have to take on changing by yourself; reach out and find a role model. Whether you know them or not, read their books, listen to their audio tapes. Success leaves clues.

Decide on a plan of action, and then take action. As you move in the desired direction, the next step will unfold. Get CDs, DVDs, read biographies and autobiographies, enroll in school and do information interviews. Start moving towards your desired dream-job. There is no climbing out of any rut, including a job rut, without taking action.

> *"If God can bring me out of poverty and despair and place me right in the middle of the life I'd always imagined, he can do the same for anyone. And that includes you. The conviction that you can change your life starts with your own thinking."*
>
> \- *Tyler Perry*
> *Actor, writer, producer, entrepreneur, and author of books including* <u>Higher Is Waiting</u>

CHAPTER 15

Facing Obstacles

"I believe that our work can be our best gift to ourselves, our friends and family, our communities—and the best expression of our purpose here on earth. Given the amount of time we spend working, failure to find meaningful, significant work is not just a minor misstep in living out God's plan; it is a deeper kind of failure that can make each day feel like living death."

- Dan Miller
<u>*No More Mondays*</u>

IDENTIFYING YOUR STRENGTHS

WHAT IF I DON'T REALLY KNOW WHAT I WANT TO DO? If you don't really know what you want to do, then your job is to discover what you think you want to do. Ask your inner child.

Remember when you were a child? What did you enjoy doing? What were you naturally inclined to and spent exorbitant amounts of time doing?

The clues of who you are, your purpose, what you were meant to be and do have been there since you were a child. There have been hints. For my daughter, Kash'shawn Johnson, it was art. As a two-year-old, she could sit for exorbitant amounts of time drawing in detail. Her girl would have eye-lashes, earrings and a necklace. Mickey Mouse looked like Queen Mickey Mouse.

My son, Deavay Tyler, had natural inclinations in the area of finances and problem solving. As an adult, his childhood interest has followed him into his adulthood skills of helping business owners increase their revenues, solve operational problems and aiding entrepreneurs in getting more solid financial footings.

For my youngest son, Donnavan Tyler, his patience, kindness, compassion and sense of fairness have become the bedrock of his career as a leader and administrator for a national Christian organization based in California.

As a child, writing seemed to follow and surface in many areas of my life. I've taught writing, attended writing conferences, ordered writing magazines, written when I was happy, sad or working through a challenging time. Writing has resurfaced again and again in seasons of my life. It's difficult to think of a time when I wasn't writing, even as a child. I've often said, "I didn't choose writing; it chose me."

What areas are you naturally strong in? What would you do for free, that is, even if you were not getting paid? What are your hobbies and interests? What do you spend your free time doing? In what areas do your friends, relatives and neighbors often seek advice or wisdom from you? Go on a search. Journal. Discover what you're naturally gifted in. What are your passions?

A MADE-UP MIND

My mom often said, "A made-up mind is a powerful weapon." You can no longer vacillate, but must make up your mind that you're going to pursue the job you love. You must decide not to let anything stop you, including the opinions of others, lack of resources, fear, or any other perceived or unperceived obstacle. As the lyrics of the child's hide-and-go-seek game say, "Ready or not, here I come."

There is power in making a decision, so decide for you there's no going back; decide there's no retreat; decide you'll never give up. Decide there's no other option: you'll continual to pursue work you love even in the face of failure and setbacks. You deserve it, you want it, and even if you haven't figured out all the *hows*, you are going to do it. Others have found a way around their failures, their hindrances, their rejections, their fears and uncertainty, and so will you. Put on your warrior's suit. Change your commitment level. Change your attitude. Sprout wings.

DETERMINATION

When you sprout your wings and change your attitude, you're not blindsided by the obstacles you face pursuing your dream job; pursuing dreams and goals requires dealing with roadblocks and detours.

Willingness to continue in spite of the roadblocks, embracing change and silencing the negative "you can't do this" head voice, requires an ongoing commitment to stretch—travel from your comfort zone and embrace change. Set your inner thermostat for pleasurable employment and refuse to turn it down; construct your action plan and act on the plan. Continue to stockpile the necessary knowledge, acquire the necessary skills and fight fear, as you take your successfully jobless journey. In the process, be willing to tweak your plans, but refuse to relinquish them.

WRONG BELIEVING

Another wall between you and the career of your preference could be your believing, and of course what you believe spills from your heart into your mouth. You just don't believe working an ideal job, though possible for others, is possible for you.

As the scripture says, "Out of the abundance of the heart, the mouth speaketh" (Matthew 12:34 KJV). Your thoughts, your belief, and the words of your mouth can separate you from joblessness. Wrong believing produces wrong thoughts, speaking and actions.

You can work on wrong believing, but it's helpful to first acknowledge that for you and your goals, wrong believing has become a hindrance.

Andrew Matthews, the author of *Follow Your Heart: Finding Purpose in Your Life and Work,* says, "It's possible to be paid to do what you love. Many of us grow up believing that work is meant to be a drag. Wrong! Millions of people have a ball at work and get paid for it."

I agree with Mr. Matthews. If you look closely, there is evidence all around you to support his observation. To help you get on the track in designing a life of joblessness, move forward by identifying and interviewing others who make money doing what they love in jobs that are a natural fit. By changing your perception, you can change your beliefs which will be beneficial in your preparation for pursuing work that aligns with your callings and passions.

LEAVING THE COMFORT ZONE

Many people are comfortable in the zone they're in and don't want to take risks. It is often said, "The devil you know is better than the devil you don't know."

A large part of the working population is risk adverse. One of the reasons is plain old fear, an issue we have previously discussed.

"I can't tolerate being in that void, unknown zone. It's like losing my footing."

Yes, part of the process in moving forward is letting go of what appears to be your security, your financial base, and your willingness to leave your comfort zone.

Strengthen your risk muscles. "You can't go to third base unless you take your foot off second base."

Everything you attempt will require taking risks, being willing to change and facing the possibility of failure. Taking chances involves risks, which can make us vulnerable to defeat, but on the other hand, risks can open us to achieving our dreams and a life far beyond what we could have possibly ever imagined.

The Bill Gates and Oprah Winfreys of life managed to take smart, calculated risks. Often the rewards outweigh the time spent in the struggle. Sometimes letting go of the familiar requires coaxing ourselves and asking, "What is the worst that could happen?" Nothing can be worse than not giving yourself permission to pursue your dreams.

FEAR OF THE DARK FAILURE ZONE

Give yourself permission to go through the dark failure zone if it's the way across the bridge. Tell yourself it's going to be okay. If you fall and bruise yourself, it's going to be okay. If you make silly mistakes, it's just a season for learning; it's going to be okay. If you have to go back in the dark-failure zone again and again, each time you'll learn something. You'll make it further across the dark forest. It's going to be okay!

How do you go into that dark-failure zone and get new strength to go back in again and again, if necessary? It is the same thing as when I decided to go into the professional real estate investment zone to support my writing-self while freeing myself from a traditional job. I submitted offer after offer. I submitted contract after contract before finally securing a property. There were times I would make 10 to 20 offers before getting one property to run with towards the finish line of securing financing. As I write this, my dark-failure notebook rests nearby where I have put my rejections. Today, however, I have obtained enough property and experiences that I'm called a professional real estate investor. It's important that you arm yourself with a spirit that refuses to give up, even when you're walking through the dark failure zone of your dreams and searching for a career you love.

> *"If you are getting up every morning and going to a job that you hate, that is not living. You're just existing."*
> *- Steve Harvey*
> *Comedian, actor, entrepreneur author of several books including Jump*

CHAPTER 16
Power in the Little

"God hides great things in little things. In every young girl, God hides a great woman; in every young boy, He hides a great man; in a small seed, He hides a big forest! A little is never inadequate if God's hands are its creator! Don't despise little things!"
- Israelmore Ayivor
Speaker and author

In the classic Aesop fable *The Lion and the Mouse,* a lion captures a mouse, who pleas for his life promising that if the lion frees him, one day he will repay him. The king of the jungle looks at the helpless little mouse and sort of chuckles asking what he could possibly do for him; still, the lion sets the mouse free.

One day, the mouse hears the lion roaring and fighting, moaning and groaning. As the mouse gets closer, he sees the lion is caught in a hunter's net. The mouse gets busy gnawing on the ropes until he sets the lion free. The lion had underestimated the power of the little mouse.

Don't underestimate the power of the little.

When the task of finding meaningful work seems overwhelming, remember, even small actions count when pursuing the job of your dreams. Stop focusing on the big things, the things you can't do, the things that seem out of reach. Focus on the little things you are able to do to inch your way to entrepreneurship or towards your dream career. Like the lion, don't underestimate the power of little things.

Inching your way in the right direction could mean getting a taste of autonomy by asking your boss if you could work from home a couple of days a week, like my computer-literate son, Kelvin Johnson, did.

Inching your way there might mean be willing to stay at your current job, but negotiating a 3 or 4-day work-week because you have built a strong enough financial base.

Personally, I inched my way out of my job by systematically taking a sabbatical leave without pay. It gave me a chance to try my wings of independence for a year, to see if I could handle not receiving a steady paycheck.

For me, gradually shifting meant bypassing opportunities to teach extra curriculum classes and not working summer school, so I could give myself the gift of time and the opportunity to build another stream of income. Eventually, the business I built completely replaced my teacher's salary. Employing incremental steps transported me from traditional employment to self-employment and to earning a living in ways that supported my authentic self.

Consider others who have turned a hobby into a money-making venture, built a home-based business, obtained or found their dream-job by consistently taking small steps. It's possible.

The scriptures remind us not to despise small beginnings (Zechariah 4:10 NLT), so if the goal of becoming jobless doesn't happen readily, continue to apply your patience and perseverance muscles knowing that gradual movement towards your dream-career outweighs no movement at all.

Delays aren't signposts of impossibilities; keep moving and taking action, even if the process seems slow and the steps you're taking are only minute. There's power in the little.

SWISS CHEESE

Take out your journal and continue planning; remember, written goals are essential. Breaking your goals into bite-size pieces and tackling one bite-size piece at a time are suggestions that motivation coaches offer to their clients when clients are confronted with overwhelming tasks. Coaches often refer to this approach as the swiss-cheese method of accomplishing goals. A little here and a little there works wonders! Raindrops create a steady flow of rain, which can create floods. Or the continual falling of snowflakes can bring a city to a snowy halt. Focused, little action steps can be powerful, so remember huge differences rest behind the little things we continuously do.

Focused effort, whether it's returning to school and taking one little class after another, or steadily building a client-base, mixed with determination and patience, can launch you towards the lifestyle and a career you can cherish.

To get started or to keep your momentum going, swiss-cheese your way to success. Remember the lesson of the lion: freedom can lie in the power of small things.

DECIDE ON YOUR BABY STEPS

Brainstorm: decide what baby steps you can take towards finding a more satisfying career. Perhaps you can volunteer in an area of your interest at first. Are you interested in the medical field?

Volunteering at a hospital at first, before applying to nursing school, might be insightful. Are you interested in journalism? Have you considered writing articles for your local community paper as a prelude to applying for journalism school? Want to open your own restaurant? Maybe by becoming a waitress at someone else's restaurant, you'll see what the business entails: management skills, organization skills and customer service skills. It's not a matter of merely being the best cook in town.

Knowledgeable, slow, directed steps will help you build income in a field that sincerely brings you joy, a field that gives you a sense of contentment and inner peace. While baby steps are suggested, getting started and being persistent is mandatory. If you ever discover you're making definitive steps, but you're going in the wrong direction, U-turns are permitted.

What happens when the momentum you've gained appears to be a false start—when what you thought would be your dream job is not your dream job after all? Don't despair, that too is part of the process. Regroup, turn around and continue moving. Gathering information about what suits you and what doesn't is part of the process. In fact, you're one step closer to discovering what you do like when you are authentic and know what jobs *don't* suit you.

Be kind, gentle and forgiving of yourself. Give yourself room to grow.

> *"Even though you haven't reached your goal yet, with each step you are getting closer. Don't think about the finish line. Enjoy the race! Don't allow yourself to become overwhelmed with how far you still have to go.*
> *Focus on one step at a time.*
> *Be grateful for how far you've come.*
> *Thank God for where you are.*
> *Keep going."*
>
> *- Tyler Perry*

Actor, film-producer and author of books, including
<u>Higher Is Waiting</u>

CHAPTER 17
Role Models of Success

"The only way to get rid of the fear of doing something is to go out and do it."
- Susan Jeffers
Author of <u>Feel the Fear and Do It Anyway</u>

MODELING ENTREPRENEURS

My friend, Janet Bell, the mother of W. Kamau Bell, a television host and comedian, encouraged her son to be his best self even before he was making sufficient income or noticeable inroads in the entertainment or media business. Before I left my teaching job and launched out into real estate and writing, I remember a profound question Janet asked me when I complained about being caught up in the clutches of the 9 to 5 world.

"If publishing is a billion-dollar industry and you want to be in it, what makes you think you can't make money in the publishing industry?"

At that time, I thought being without a traditional job meant being broke and frustrated, I doubted I could make money in a field I loved, and for me, launching from traditional employment seemed too risky. I dismissed the thought that many people thrived without getting a paycheck every two weeks, including my friend Janet.

Work if you love to; work if it feeds you soul. Work if it's your passion, but if it's not, maybe it's time to consider entrepreneurship, and embrace the opportunity to uniquely design your income producing source. Perhaps working is not for you. Perhaps it separates you from your dream, an area where you could financially and emotionally thrive. Have you ever considered becoming an entrepreneur? Have you considered the number of successful people who are not tied to a time clock, who can make money in their sleep with passive income and who choose to work independently instead of working a job?

If you didn't have any monetary needs, would you show up at your job on Mondays? Have you thought about why the first thing many lottery winners do is quit their jobs?

I personally *do not* believe your way to freedom and financial freedom is through the lottery; however, when you use your God-given gifts to serve others and produce an income and live a whole and satisfactory life, you have won life's lottery.

OUT-OF-THE-BOX LIVING

If 70 to 80 percent of employees are not truly happy with their jobs, what prevents them from changing careers or starting their own business?

People have built thriving lawn care business, child care facilities, cleaning services, consulting businesses—the list is endless.

When you consider turning your hobbies and interests into a business, you might think it will require an investment of your time, money and energy, and you are certainly right.

Business ownership can be risky; being a business owner requires a host of skills including ingenuity, discipline, risk-taking skills, leadership skills, problem-solving and decision-making skills and money management skills. It often requires all you have, then more; entrepreneurship offers ample opportunities for growth. Becoming a business owner means slaying traditional thinking and living, and it requires you to engage your out-of-box-thinking and living skills. It absolutely isn't a life for the fearful.

If you decide to join the circle of entrepreneurs, don't expect everyone to cheer you on. Many people have adopted traditional ways of thinking, and entrepreneurship isn't a blip on their radar. Some of your friends and family members may even feel their job is to save you from such a dangerous mission. Others will be envious, and some have forever pledged their allegiance to traditional employment and refuse to even consider changing their paradigm. This, of course, doesn't mean they are awful people.

To love the specific work you were put on earth to do, perhaps after much deliberation, you have decided to create it. Previously, business ownership might have seemed like an impossible dream, but keep dreaming anyway. Allow your soul and heart to embrace the dream of entrepreneurship; even if it's doesn't appear immediately on the horizon, don't dismiss the possibility. Like others, it can be a dream that you can step into—if not all at once, then gradually.

Remember: with God, all things are possible. You too can find a job that aligns to your true goals and purposes, even if it requires creating your own.

If you want to explore entrepreneurship, there are organizations like the Small Business Association and the Joseph Center (in Forest Park, Illinois), who can help usher you through the door. Surround yourself with others who have refused to settle and have found profitable, meaningful and pleasurable work by becoming entrepreneurs.

ROLE MODELS

Being around people who are visionaries and fearless when it comes to living an authentic, happy life can be contagious. It is hard to live your best life (thanks, Joel Osteen) if your daily lifestyle doesn't support your best work. After all, considering the time we spend preparing for, commuting to and being at work, how can we ignore job satisfaction?

One step in creating income doing what we love is by spending time with or by reading about others who prospered without traditional jobs. It's great if you personally know or regularly associate with a group of these people, but if not, you can meet them through books, audio tapes and even podcasts. When you do not have access to the local store owner, the lady who owns her own antique shop or the car dealership owner, find other ways, through conferences, trainings, community organizations or the media, to surround yourself with achievers.

Have you noticed how many people we consider financially secure continue to come to work because their work feeds their soul, provides a service and is enjoyable? What makes you think you don't deserve to be one of them? Retrain your beliefs, re-frame your thought life and refrain from saying, "I could never do that." Yes, it's possible to work for yourself, create your own business or source of income. If you decide to be employed, find a job where you can be happy and fulfilled. It's possible for you to join the ranks of those who pushed traditional thinking, traditional employment and their fears aside and are succeeding in making significant income while doing work they love.

"I predict that if you pick a business that you love, and you faithfully spend your hour doing the key parts of the business, that within two years you will be well on your way to complete financial independence."
- Richard Carlson
<u>*Don't Worry, Make Money*</u>

CHAPTER 18

The Process

"Look at how many people are doing work they don't like at all--don't give their best, and aren't proud of. For your sake and the sake of the world, you must follow your gifts. One question is: where do they lead? The other is: when will you go after them?"

- Barbara Sher
Author of <u>Live the Life You Love</u>

CONQUERING THE TROLL

In the classic Norwegian child's tale *Three Billy Goats Gruff,* there's a troll preventing the goats from crossing over a bridge, sabotaging their journey to their feeding ground.

What stops you along your pathway to a more satisfying job? What's your personal troll? Is it fear, lack of resources, lack of finances, lack of information? You need to identify your troll so you can get a plan of action for defeating him. Whether your troll is real or imagined, it's still a big, old, ugly monster that pops its ugly head out every time you decide to cross your bridge to joblessness. How are you going to deal with your troll?

Is your troll a mountain of debt? A lack of resources? Indecisiveness? A lack of support? An inefficient knowledge base?

Trolls make the task of being jobless without sacrificing a satisfying lifestyle seem impossible. But look around you; how many others have managed to defeat their ugly trolls?

Identify the actions you can take to begin moving across your troll-guarded bridge. Perhaps it's time to research. Take a trip to the library to explore how you can turn your hobby, passion or interest into income-producing opportunities. Or maybe your initial step in bridge-crossing could be a commitment to stop your shopping madness, cut up your credit cards or write a get-out-of-debt plan. You decide. Key steps, however, are to begin and to persist.

PREPARE TO FIGHT

On your journey towards job satisfaction, don't be blindsided when other trolls arrive, but keep traveling. As you move along your path, you will gain experience in slaying or outwitting your trolls, so you'll be better equipped to handle them. Even if you feel like David and your Goliath or giant is humongous, move towards the monster boldly, knowing God knows how to slay giants, monsters and trolls, and by faith, you know He has your back.

If you've consistently pulled out your jobless journal and reflected and planned, by now your vision is starting to take shape. You are beginning to see the value and power in written plans. It's a battle trying to redesign your work-life, but by gathering tools of knowledge and resources, and by assembling your team, you realize slaying your trolls doesn't have to be a solo act. You're also beginning to see the value of action and are determined to act, even when you can only take baby steps in crossing your bridge, but you know baby steps count, even scary baby steps. You are prepared to fight to keep moving, and you have decided that even if the progress is slow, you'll continue and fight. For you, quitting is not an option.

DOING THE RIGHT THING

One of Spike Lee's first works was *Do the Right Thing*. When we hear this title, we think Lee is telling the listener to make a good moral decision.

For those of you who know the importance of choosing the right career path, *Do the Right Thing* can also become a call to pursue your purpose or the right job for you. Doing the right thing is critical for success seekers; for when we do the right thing, we function in the area that caters to our gifts and talents, which is a catalyst for the commitment and passion that leads us to success. Perhaps like me, you're tottering, the progress seems slow and tears are welling up in your eyes, yet you persist. After I complained about how difficult it was to get my college degree, my friend Rubie Stepney said, "If it was easy, everyone would do it." But for me during that season in my life, getting my degree was my right thing, so I continued to study, fight and move forward.

Despite difficulties, continue to move in the direction of your dreams, and do what you know is the right thing for you.

ENLIST HELP

One can put a thousand to flight; two can put 10,000 to flight. After you have identified your troll, adjusted your attitude and decided how you go about defeating your troll, like the main character in Three Billy Goats Gruff, get help. The billy goat turned to an older brother to help him make it safely across the bridge where the troll lingered.

Bishop T. D. Jakes talks about the importance of building a team around a project or idea. Getting a mentor and enlisting help to cross your bridge is invaluable.

I have managed to continue building my knowledge-base and solving problems in the real estate field because of the support and encouragement from associates and friends. Relationship building is of utmost importance as Pastor Mike Wilkins, the CEO of SPAA (Speakers Publishers Authors Association), often tells its members. CJ and Shelley Hitz, creators of Christian Book Academy, say the same things using a different shift in their words: If you want to go far, build a team.

You will hit tough times as you take on the challenge to change. A key piece of information that someone already has can make a difference in you being successful or failing in your endeavors.

When I reached a certain plateau but decided to take my business in a different direction and become more of a sophisticated investor, seasoned real estate investors Stephanie Windham and Bill Rodney surfaced and were ready to hold my shaking real estate hands.

Whatever direction you choose, whatever lessons you still have to learn, whatever wisdom you need, don't underestimate the value of mentors. Look, because they're all around. Someone has done what you're trying to do, and they are probably very willing to let you glean from their knowledge base. ASK.

> *"Everyone has one person who either means the most to them or was the first to influence, train, or manage them. No one succeeds alone. No one."*
> *- Gary Keller and Jay Papapsan*
> *Authors of The One Thing*

Chapter 19
Financial Obstacles

"Sometimes we buy a lot of toys to take our mind off the fact that we hate our job."
- Andrew Matthews
Author of <u>Follow Your Heart:
Finding Purpose in Your Life and Work</u>

CROSSING YOUR RED SEA

My bother-in-law Robert Holder, Jr. often found himself caught in the grips of job change. At first it seemed to surprise my sister, Pat, but she and Robert are quick learners. They immediately began to store more resources away. Whether a job transition was thrust upon him or he decided to leave an unsuitable job, the couple was able to put up their financial umbrella.

Decades later, Robert and Pat have comfortably retired from full-time jobs. They fill their schedule with travel, meeting with their financial planner, meeting with friends and deciding who to be a blessing to.

Their financial decisions and the grace of God have helped them navigate through working careers that were sometimes turbulent. They learned to invest, live below their means and be discreet and wise when it came to spending. Accolades to them and other couples who positioned themselves for financial success. Robert sometimes works two days a week, a part-time job at a local golf club, for pure satisfaction, and he gets to play golf free.

FINANCIAL LITERACY

One of the major issues hindering many from seeking job satisfaction is finances. Lack and limited assets could be how your troll looks, peering out from under the bridge, separating you from your goals. An outspoken advocate on getting your finances together is Robert Kiyosaki, whose journey has taken him from homelessness to becoming a multi-millionaire. In his book, *Why the Rich Are Getting Richer,* Kiyosaki states, "Financial illiteracy causes a person to hate life. Millions are stuck in jobs they hate, not earning the money they want and need to earn. It is estimated that 70% of all American workers actually hate their jobs. They sell their most valuable asset—their life—for a paycheck."

BECOME DEBT ADVERSE

Emotions can become deterrents in seeking your dream job, especially fear in regards to your finances. It's difficult for you to envision how you're going to fill the financial gap as you transition. At times, frustration crops up, turning into excessive spending, buying toys like a new car, computer equipment, a new sound system, the latest big screen television; or taking lavish vacations; or purchasing designer clothes, bags and shoes. Your closets burst at the seams while your heart grows emptier. You fill your life with gadgets, activities, and other pacifiers, hoping they'll take the place of your true desires. Can shopping sprees answer your heart's cry, or only put you in more debt and delay your true dreams and goals?

Our environment exposes us to messages that don't support finding meaningful work, but it does support credit cards use. By adopting beliefs that draw you towards purpose-filled work, you become aware of the daily messages bombarding the media, which are at odds with your mission. It's important to protect a mindset that directs you towards visions of becoming debt-free, of building cash reserves and opportunity funds and obtaining your goals.

In his book *The Total Money Makeover,* financial guru Dave Ramsey states, "If you keep doing the same things, you will keep getting the same results. You are where you are right now financially as a sum total of the decisions you've made to this point."

One of the main hindrances for people pursuing work they love is lack of finances. We are not helpless when it comes to our finances; realize this as you prepare to transition. Stop seeing yourself as a victim in regards to money, decide to stop spending frivolously, get control of your finances and apply needed delayed gratification. Learn to say no to excessive spending.

The questions of finances also surfaced for me personally when I decided to change careers; it is not an obstacle easily ignored. I had to examine ways to launch myself in the right financial path since I was determined that nothing would get in the way of my pursuit. I realized others had navigated through the dark forest of lack, through overspending and around financial barriers, and so would I. Success leaves clues—all I had to do was to look for and follow the breadcrumbs.

25 FINANCIAL TIPS

Preparing to answer your jobless call means getting your financial house in order. Here are 25 recommendations to assist you in your journey.

1. Study. Become more financially literate. Listen to Dave Ramsey, Gary Keesee, Susan Orman or some other financial guru on YouTube or invest time in reading books on finances. If you are in kindergarten or second grade when it comes to your financial knowledge, you don't have to remain there. Grow.
2. Listen to audio tapes. While commuting, take time to listen to financially-based audio tapes to help improve your financial literacy. Your local library houses an abundance of tapes on many subjects, including finances, which you can borrow for free.
3. Manage your spending. Get a spending plan. This is a friendly way of saying you'll need some kind of budget.
4. Pay off and stop using credit cards. It's easier to navigate the employment waters when you're not anchored to debt. Good expert advice is, "If you're out of money, stop spending." Become debt-free and debt-adverse.
5. Save for your job transition. Saving requires delayed gratification. Say *no* to today's toys, so you can build tomorrow's future. Pay yourself and pay yourself first.
6. Make saving a habit. Build reserves for emergencies and for opportunities, and add money into your reserve account automatically. When you get raises on your current job, save your increases.
7. Explore your money attitudes. What money beliefs have you adopted that no longer work for you? Do you have a scarcity mentality? "Money doesn't grow on trees." "Some people are always going to be poor." "My money is short, like me." Realign your thinking and set financial goals that will undergird your long-term goals of finding career and financial freedom.

8. Abandon your keeping-up-with-the-Joneses lifestyle. The Joneses probably have credit card debt and are living above their means. In his book *The Total Money Makeover*, financial guru Dave Ramsey says, "We have permanently quit keeping up with the Joneses, because the Joneses are broke."
9. Drive cheaper. Pay off your car note or don't sign for a car note in the first place. Get a car that doesn't flash and pay cash.
10. Find a financial mentor, someone to hold you financially accountable. Identify a mentor who has achieved a level of financial stability who will encourage you and share wisdom as you set your own financial bar higher.
11. Discipline yourself. Are you wrestling with a shopping addiction? Ask yourself: "Do my financial goals require that I stay out of stores or stop shopping online?" Then find a less financial-taxing way to deal with frustration, boredom or the need for entertainment.
12. Make wiser financial decisions. Get rid of the whistles and bells on your cable. Try getting just a basic cable package or forego cable altogether.
13. Check out your insurance costs. Is it time to change insurance companies? Is it time to raise your deductible? Talk to your agent or an insurance broker about lowering your premiums.
14. Instead of visiting Starbucks, invest in to-go cups and a Keurig or another simple-to-use coffee maker.
15. Planning your meals and cooking at home can save you hundreds of dollars each month. Learn your way around the kitchen or invest in a slow cooker. Besides, home-cooked meals are more nutritious.

16. Step back and examine your lifestyle. Is there an area, like going out with your friends weekly, that's costly and can delay your debt-freedom goals? Putting a brake on bad financial habits will give you more resources for building an emergency fund or stock piling cash in your opportunity fund.
17. Look for overlooked areas in your life where you can apply delayed gratification. Tell yourself that when you reach your work and financial goals, then you can afford to splurge somewhat, but now is not the time.
18. Identify your financial weaknesses. Do you tend to watch the shopping channel and eventually pull out you credit card when a sale you just can't resist is offered? Instead, turn off the television and go for a walk.
19. Putting your savings plan on automatic is one of the best ways to become financially sound.
20. Decide you're going to take control of your money. Organize your system. Do you have a special place to put bills and invoices when they come in? Do you pay your utilities, insurances and other bills on time? The bottom line is to get a grip on your finances; lead your financial parade.
21. If you get off track financially, get back on. Be determined to do what it takes to free yourself to pursue your dreams and goals.
22. Realign your thinking. Sacrificing now is merely a temporary inconvenience, not a life-sentence of lack and self-deprivation.
23. Be determined to create gun money—money you can shoot into your future that can be used to purchase appreciating assets. With all the gun money you'll accumulate, sometime in the future, you can buy plenty of butter items—items that

have little value after their purchase like fancy purses, brand-name shoes, designer dresses and a little trinket here and there. Right now, however, is your season of reorganizing and gathering your resources.
24. Remember your goal is not to live in lack but to give yourself financial room to reach forward towards finding work that provides you with both emotional and financial rewards. Obtaining a long-term goal for a short-term sacrifice is worth it.
25. If necessary, drive Uber, work as a waitress, deliver pizzas, sell items on eBay, or stop taking a yearly vacation to build a stronger financial base. Some financial experts encourage their audience to engage in *side-hustles* to increase their income and have more resources to direct towards obtaining their financial freedom.

LOOK AHEAD

It is impressive when people from other nations immigrate to the United States, and often with limited language skills, build lucrative businesses and provide an affluent lifestyle for their families. Their foresight and sacrifice open doors of opportunities for generational wealth.

Your ability to face your challenges and sacrifice to obtain work you love will leave pathways for the future generations to follow. My grandmother used to say, "What we do is much louder than our words." By tapping into your pool of hope, resiliency and faith you become a role model for endurance and change, so never look back or go back, even when the journey is slow and bumpy. You too can leave generational footprints, and possibly generational wealth.

America offers an abundance of opportunities, and even in its biggest challenges and worst times, people from other nations see our advantages.

Although the coronavirus hit our nation hard, with deaths, business closings and job loss, my attitude was, *we will come back; Americans are resilient.*

When my neighbor said, "I can't wait to go back to normal," I thought, we will never be able to go back to things being like they were before. There are times there's no portal to the "old" normal; a new normal looms on the horizon.

When you make up your mind to change careers and to reposition your thinking and yourself, you have stepped in a world of a new normal. Your issues, financial setbacks and hindrances, and what seems like the darkest seasons in your life, can merely be the cocoon from which you're being transformed from being a caterpillar into a butterfly.

The season of the coronavirus has highlighted the importance of having your financial life in order and not taking the time you've been given on this earth for granted. That's why it's more important than ever before to do work you love so you can live a good life.

Don't count yourself out. You have what it takes to cross over your financial Red Sea and into a world of goodness, possibility and prosperity. Believe in yourself. Manage your finances. Be willing to hold on to your dreams despite the challenges. At first, you'll see little wins begin to blossom, but before you know it, pleasurable and big wins will emerge.

> *"A lot of folks have no choice but to work at soul-sucking jobs, because they need the money. Believe me, I took some pretty dreary gigs that did nothing for me but pay my bills so I could keep a roof over my head. That's why I know it's not always easy to aim higher when it comes to*

work. But once you set your sights on a meaningful goal, you can put yourself on the path. That's the only way higher can be reached—by moving toward it."
- Tyler Perry
Author of <u>Higher Is Waiting</u>

Chapter 20
Stretch Your Wings

"Anything that we do for years that doesn't match the inner imprint of our gifting will eventually become monotonous and routine, ritualistic and frustrating."
- T. D. Jakes
Pastor, filmmaker and author of books including <u>Instinct</u>

I once saw a sign that said: "Let's just pretend it's Saturday." I smiled feeling like I understood how the sign's creator felt. Years ago, I could hardly wait for the week's end; I think the restaurant chain TGI Friday—Thank God It's Friday—was created for me. On Fridays, I would unwind after a full week of getting my kids to school, running a single-parent household, and working a job that no longer fed my soul. Mind you, I was an excellent teacher, yet my gut knew that it was time for a change. As a well-meaning friend pointed out to me, I didn't wait to get Monday morning blues, but I was guilty of getting Sunday morning blues. My friend was wrong: I was guilty of the Saturday night blues. My weekends were far too short.

For many years, entrepreneurship had been tapping me on the shoulder. My bills, responsibilities, family members and fears warned me not to listen. But I finally mustered up the courage to turn around and pay attention.

Job dissatisfaction has a way of spreading outside the boundaries of Monday through Friday and creeping into your weekends too. It affects your attitude, spending habits, relationships and even your health; it definitely demands not to be ignored.

EXCUSES

A prominent black agricultural scientist and inventor George Washington Carver once said, "Ninety-nine percent of the failures come from people who have the habit of making excuses."

You give yourself a mountain of excuses for not changing directions when your job choice no longer lines up with your authentic self, purposes and gifts. The mountain of reasons can almost seem insurmountable.

Inwardly you protest, while the call to change careers grows louder and louder until you can't outrun what has transitioned from a loud voice to a piercing scream.

Transitioning into an independent income-producing adult can be difficult enough without carrying along the dream of pleasurable and passion-filled work. There are some factors that you may choose to ignore but can resurface later as you settle for work that you are not uniquely designed to do, but one day you're forced to look at yourself in the employment mirror.

Could the real reason for working a less than ideal job be connected to your unwillingness to take risks? Do you believe if you turn down one job, a more suitable job may not come along? Do you really trust yourself? Trust your abilities? A better question still is: do you trust God?

Maybe a combination of factors prevents you from stretching your wings and finding enjoyable employment or opting to become an entrepreneur.

By this point, you have revisited your childhood dreams and journaled to unearth what you think your ideal work should be. You've built your courage muscles and found others—whether in organizations, in books or in your community—that have stretched their wings of success.

If you haven't begun your journey, take action; now is the time to start. Faith without works is dead. (James 2: 26 KJV) It's time for you to soar. Enough analyzing, enough thinking about it; it's time to be about it.

There's no failure that haunts our soul like the failure of not trying. As the fairy-tale of *The Ugly Duckling* goes, it is only when we start seeing that we are different, we don't belong with the ducks, that we realize we are eagles and we begin to stretch our wings to fly.

In my first award-winning book *Stretch Your Wings: Famous Black Quotations for Teens*, co-authored with Janet Bell, there is a quotation by Ronald McNair, the astronaut who was killed in the Challenger spaceship in 1986. "Whether or not you reach your goals in life depends entirely on how well you prepare for them and how badly you want them.... You're eagles! Stretch your wings and fly to the sky!"

It's important that we see ourselves as the eagles we are and know that we don't belong in the barnyards of life.

The book encourages young people to consider their choices, including the work they enjoy and are naturally gifted to do. Pat Campbell, a diversity marketing, strategic planner, is quoted. "Find out what you love to do, and then figure out how to make money doing it." What great advice!

Even before he was nationally and internationally known, before fame had visited him or before he had some level of financial security, Louis Armstrong felt at home because he was being productive in the arena of his natural calling, gifts and talents. According to this renowned jazz musician, "When I got my first job in New Orleans playing in a honky-tonk...I was seventeen, and it was the same as Carnegie Hall to me."

The celebrated Colin Powell, the first African American to chair the joint Chiefs of Staff, and a retired U.S. Army general, once stated, "In class, I stumbled through math, fumbled through physics, and... even enjoyed geology. (However), all I ever looked forward to was ROTC." There are tale-tell signs even in our youth of what our purpose and callings are, where we will feel at home when it comes to a career, what we were put on this earth to do.

Maybe you are a late bloomer when it comes to discovering your life calling—the job for which you were uniquely designed do. Perhaps you are like Ed Dwight.

Dwight, a renowned sculptor, stated, "It took from the time I was seventeen...'til I was forty-five to make the decision that (art) was what I really wanted to do. I couldn't live the rest of my life without doing it."

W.E.B. DuBois, founder of the NAACP and an author, said, "The thing which has been the secret of whatever I have done is the fact that I have been able to earn a living by doing the work which I wanted to do and the work that the world needed done."

In *Stretch Your Wings*, Herman Cain, CEO of Godfather Pizza, was quoted. "Success if not the key to happiness. Happiness is the key to success. If you love what you are doing, you will be successful."

The book was distributed nation-wide and received publicity throughout the United States. The Catholic Schools system chose the book to be on their list of recommended readings. *Stretch Your Wings*, which ended up in a youth juvenile home and even in the prison system, was a message to both youth and adults, but it is still a message to me, a public-school teacher at the time of its publication.

Making good choices and answering your soul's calling will heighten the likelihood of your success. Financial gains and job satisfaction increase when you do what you love and when your chosen career reflects the areas of your strengths, talents and gifting. Sure, it takes courage, but it will be well worth the price you pay.

Whether 12, 18, 34 or 50, there's no substitute for stretching your wings and taking flight.

> *"Passion for something leads to disproportionate time practicing or working at it. That time spent eventually translates to skill, and when skill improves, results improve. Better results generally lead to more enjoyment, and more passion and more time is invested. It can be a virtuous cycle all the way to extraordinary results."*
> *- Gary Keller and Jay Papasan*
> *Authors of <u>The One Thing</u>*

Chapter 21
Employing Our Faith

"No matter how gifted you were at receiving income one way, it doesn't mean that you can't unearth the creativity and passion to receive it another way."
- T. D. Jakes
Pastor, filmmaker and author of books including <u>Instinct</u>

By employing your faith, you can overcome fear and find the courage and confidence you need to pursue pleasurable work.

Faith says I can do all things through Christ who strengthens me. (Philippians 4: 13 KJV). Faith says you are more than a conqueror (Romans 8:37 KJV). Faith says God hasn't given you a spirit of fear (2 Timothy 1:7 KJV). When you don't see a way out, you can *faith* your way out.

Employing your faith helps silence the self-doubt, the obstacles, the mountains and the fears standing between you and your goal of having your dream job. By faith, you can believe in your capability of finding work you love and are gifted at. The scripture speaks of abundant life (John 10:10 KJV). How can you live a joyful, peaceful, abundant life without engaging in work that you're passion about and that is profitable?

Changing career direction has opened doors of opportunities and streams of income for me that were not available before. I have the freedom of spending my time, energy and creativity doing work that's uniquely suited to me. I've had to *faith* myself to this position; the times I've asked for divine wisdom, help and favor has been countless. Failure and fear, at times, seemed to be waiting around the next corner determined to snatch me, but by faith I persisted.

The fact that I'm able to work in the area of my passion and still have a lucrative income has surprised me. It has motivated me to write this book, which is designed to give hope to those who are less than satisfied with their current work situation and want to go in a different direction. It is possible to spend hours working and feel like you are not working at all but just having fun. When you are doing work you truly love, those hours in the workplace can actually seem like endless play. Pursuing a job you would do even if there was no pay involved enables you to put away clock-watching, frustration, discontentment, and glass ceilings and stare in the face of passion.

JOBLESSNESS

When we watch Michael Jordan on the basketball court, Tiger Woods playing golf, Oprah Winfrey interviewing, Denzel Washington or Meryl Streep acting, Michael Jackson or Phil Driscoll performing, we're watching art in action and genius at work. We are witnessing joblessness and people doing what they were uniquely called to do.

When ballet dancer Misty Copeland glides through the air powerfully and gracefully, it testifies of the years and thousands of hours she's spent practicing. Gifts come alive with persistence and practice. Joblessness is a dream you breathe life into; joblessness just doesn't fall into your lap. Pursuing your dream is the best way to ensure that you find work that employs your strengths, passion and gifts. Countless artists, musicians, entrepreneurs, entertainers, athletes, single parents, students, and educators have solicited divine help through prayer before entering the arena to utilize their gifts. Faith, work, prayer and discipline are powerful combinations. Faith without work is unprofitable. Have you started your jobless journal? Have you explored work in an area in which you are keenly interested? Have you begun volunteering in a field that excites you? Have you decided how you're going to build your skills? Have you applied for a class in the area of your interest? Have you identified a mentor?

God blesses what we do. Are you a doer or merely a thinker? If you have not begun a plan of action to cross the bridge from where you are to where you want to be, it's not too late to start. Faith is important, but action is too. The scripture says: "For as the body without the spirit is dead, so faith without works is dead also." (James 2:26 NKJV), and, "Show me your faith without your works, and I will show you my faith by my works." (James 2:18 NKJV).

Begin to take action now; by no means should you sit back and merely dream. Dream creatively. Dream with confidence. But most of all, dream by doing. Put feet to your dreams.

For those of you who know the importance of adding faith to your pursuit, consider the following scriptures. Meditate on them and say them out loud. Add these and other scriptures that have special meaning to you in your journal.

- "If you abide in me, and my words abide in you, you will ask what ye will, and it shall be done unto you." (John 15:7 KJV)
- "I will lift up mine eyes unto the hills, from whence cometh my help. My help cometh from the Lord, which made heaven

and earth. He will not suffer thy foot to be moved." (Psalm 121:1-3 KJV)
- "Fear thou not; for I am with thee: be not dismayed; for I am you God: I will strengthen thee; yea, I will help thee; yea, I will uphold thee with the right hand of my righteousness." (Isaiah 41:10 KJV)
- "In God have I put my trust: I will not be afraid. What can man do to me?" (Psalms 56:11 NKJV)
- "The Lord is my light and my salvation; whom shall I fear? The LORD is the strength of my life; of whom shall I be afraid?" (Psalm 27:1 KJV)
- "Now thanks be unto God, which always causeth us to triumph in Christ...." (2 Corinthians 2:14 KJV)
- "Yet in all these things we are more than conquerors." (Romans 8:37 NKJV)
- "And all things, whatsoever ye shall ask in prayer, believing, ye will receive." (Matthew 21:22 KJV)
- "But my God shall supply all your need according to His riches in glory by Christ Jesus." (Philippians 4:19 KJV)
- "Now unto him that is able to do exceeding abundantly above all that we ask or think, according to the power that worketh in us." (Ephesians 3:20 KJV)

> *"I can tell you why people often feel depressed and defeated about their lives. They were created to be so much; yet they live their lives on such a low level. Therefore, they are miserable and feel as if they are going nowhere with their lives. They are living so far below the FIRST WORDS God ever spoke to man that their souls have become sullen and sad. Something inside them knows they were born to be and to do so much more than what they are experiencing in their low-level existence."*
> *- Rick Renner*
> *Minister and author of books including* <u>Secret Dreams</u>

Chapter 22

Keep Flying

"There are hundreds of thousands of people who have overcome both internal and external obstacles to become successful doing work they love. If people can cultivate self-respect and inner security and develop a commitment to their own talents, they can earn as much money as they need, or want. This is true success..."
- Marsha Sinetar
Author of <u>Do What You Love, The Money Will Follow</u>

Joblessness is a continual mindset. Once you've started to soar in the directions of your passions and dreams, you'll want to stay in flight. Staying in flight requires checking your attitudes and beliefs and maintaining and polishing the plane that has moved you from desire to reality. Routinely check your flight instruments: the people you are around, the voice in your head, and your financial habits.

Enjoy the fruits of your hard work. Your ability to make money while doing what you love may even surprise you, but now you know it's possible.

One of the fruits of answering your unique calling will be an increase in joy in other areas of your life. Your newfound happiness and confidence levels are bound to overflow and spill into other parts of your life—your spiritual, emotional, and social lives and even into your health. Say *yes* to the journey. Continue to embrace the principles that work.

JOBLESS TUNE-UPS

We don't drive cars without doing tire-pressure checks, oil changes, tune-ups and minor repairs. As you've moved down the highway and taken your journey to joyful work, your courage, persistence, discipline, resilience and resourcefulness muscles have all grown stronger and have ushered you into unprecedented success. You've broken through your past preconceived limitations into a realm you never thought possible. You know this is just the beginning, so commit to continuing to build, review and renew.

There will be other seasons, challenges and new horizons to tackle ahead. As you transform, new challenges will unfold, but now you have an array of transformative tools at your disposal. You have experience slaying giants and dealing with trolls; there's no room for stagnation.

Terri Savelle Foy credits listening to positive motivational messages to changing her life. Continue to invest time during your morning routine and commute to listen to inspirational messages. Never forget that real wealth starts between your ears, so prune and guard your thoughts. Remember, champions act and think differently; nourish your inner champion and persist in your growth. Cherish your mentors. Drink from their cups of wisdom, experiences and advice; they are farther along than you in the journey, and your pursuit hasn't ended yet.

Just as your car's maintenance program is important, so is your personal maintenance program. Some of the same actions that brought you to being joyfully employed will keep you there and help you set the bar higher as you seek to achieve your future goals.

ON THE OTHER SIDE OF THE BRIDGE

You have learned the importance of taking action to achieve your dreams, even in the face of discomfort. Crossing to the other side of the bridge is not painless, and it often requires some type of sacrifice on the traveler's part. You've lightened your backpack by discarding mindsets, financial habits and a slew of other obstacles that can weigh a person down.

You've crossed over several bridges and have dealt with the trolls, but remember, even if you've found your ideal job or have successfully created your uniquely designed business, there will be other bridges to cross. Eventually, you're bound to face more trolls.

Be encouraged! By pursuing the career or business of your choice, you've already built muscles to help you deal with the trolls: muscles of courage, patience; determination, self-insightfulness, resilience, discipline and persistence. These muscles are invaluable as you continue your journey.

In becoming the person you've grown into, you have also become creative, resourceful and have built a strong spiritual foundation. You have grown in your ability to self-nurture and build meaningful inroads into a community that supports and honors your contributions. Overall, you stand back and look at yourself knowing you are much better for the obstacles and challenges you've faced. You've grown in your ability to trust yourself, believe in yourself and listen to your guiding inner voice. The skills you've developed will help usher you into greater seasons in your future; you've blossomed.

Continue to record your thoughts, reflections and directions. Keep journaling. You've become skillful at planning and implementing the plans; your journal will show your progress—a progress that at times will even amaze you. Your thinking and behavior have shifted so that sometimes you don't recognize that self-directed, self-assured person you're looking at in the mirror.

Though the growth journey never ends, you know you're moving in the right direction for accomplishing your dreams and answering your personal callings; you're not willing to take *no* for an answer.

You've wrapped yourself in a coat of courage to ward off winds of fear and uncertainty that once caused you to shiver and remain in place. Your confidence level has grown tremendously, and your thinking has shifted so that you hardly recognize your inner landscape. You know you have what it takes to be brave and to continue to forge ahead.

Take time to celebrate where you are and your personal growth. Reflect on your strengths and think about ways you've grown. Cheer yourself on when faced with other bridges and trolls; it's just part of life.

When you experience setbacks, reassure yourself; you moved through obstacles towards a meaningful career or entrepreneurship before, you have what it takes, and if you need to, you'll do it again. If anyone in this world is deserving to work the job of their dream and pursue their calling, why not you? Cheers.
Bravo for you!

> *"When we spend our lives waiting until we're perfect or bulletproof before we walk into the arena, we ultimately sacrifice relationships and opportunities that may not be recoverable, we squander our precious time, and we turn our backs on our gifts, those unique contributions that only we can make."*
> - Brené Brown
> Research professor and speaker who focuses on vulnerability, worthiness, shame and courage; she is also the author of several books including, <u>Daring Greatly</u>

Chapter 23
Jobless Affirmations

"When your Faith-in-Myself Muscle is strong, your self-esteem is high. You believe in yourself. You're kind to yourself. Your self-talk -the conversations in your head supports you and helps you to achieve your goals."
- Lisa Nichols
Entrepreneur, speaker and author of books including <u>No Matter What! 9 Steps to Living the Life You Love</u>

When looking for permission to pursue more pleasurable work, the most important person you can count on for support is *you*. Give yourself permission to pursue your dream-job; change your self-talk; affirm that you are deserving; become your own cheerleader. Be self-supporting and encouraging and mentally reposition yourself for success by changing your paradigm and reframing your beliefs. Stop buying into the myth of inadequacy, because you are capable of accomplishing your goals. Yes, you have what it takes!

I journaled to give myself permission to redesign my work-life. Journaling helped me to resist the subtle reasonings of my negative inner-voice and to honor my ambitions by giving myself my own seal-of-approval. If I don't honor my soul's callings, my passions, and who God made me to be, who will? Affirmations were my way of building my jobless confidence and encouraging myself. The positive declarations helped me to clean-up my thinking; to do mental housekeeping; to believe in my capabilities; to pay attention to my inner longings; to listen and value my desires; and most importantly, to continue building the courage muscles I needed to change.

Writing your own affirmations will be a valuable use of your time as you prepare yourself for new work options. The following 72 affirmations are from my personal journal and will be helpful in getting you started. Feel free to adapt and incorporate the affirmations and redesign them to make them uniquely your own.

1. **Happiness:** I deserve to be happy and when I am not, I can look within to see why I am not satisfied with my job, relationships or life. When I'm not content, or lack peace inside, I can ask myself *why,* and I really do know the answer.

2. **Inner Voice**: If I'm screaming inside that I don't want to go to a job, I can't bear to work the job for another year, week or moment, why do I refuse to listen to my inner voice? What makes me think that inner voice is wrong? Why would I try to silence it? I need to pay attention to my inner voice, not muffle it.

3. **Change:** Taking a new road, going on a new journey, and taking a new direction in life can be scary. But when change was forced upon me in the past (through divorce, through a loss or death), I might have gone kicking and screaming, but I went and adapted. In some ways, life even got better.

    Change isn't necessarily bad; change can be good. It can enhance my life. I don't have to fear change; I can welcome change. I have the strength, resiliency and courage, not only to "go" through change but to "grow" through change.

4. **Provision**: Where God leads, He provides. Even when I face some financial roadblocks, I will hold on to my faith and believe that God is a God of provision. If He is leading me in a specific direction, He will provide what I need to be sustained.

5. **Expressing Growth**: I'm growing, and I need to allow myself room to express my growth, even if it entails getting a new job or starting a new business, and letting go of a job that no longer suits me.

6. **Abundance:** The world shouts out that it is a place of abundance, so what experiences have caused me to hear the whispers of poverty? I deserve the abundance that God created on earth for me to have and enjoy. The scriptures said, He came that I might have abundant life (John 10:10 KJV). Anything less than abundant life is not acceptable.

7. **Storehouse:** I am a storehouse of abilities, talents and ideas, many of which have never been cultivated. I am a storehouse of abundance, an abundance of possibilities.

8. **Welcome Change**: I welcome change. Who says change has to be bad? There are some very positive things about change. Change helps me meet new people, have new experiences and even learn about myself, my risk-taking skills, my comfort level.

9. **Embrace Change:** A better lifestyle, productivity and a greater quality of life for mankind has been gift-wrapped in the paper of change. Change has ushered in modern-day inventions, and it has fathered the technology age we are a part of. Even when I am met with resistance and my what-ifs inner dialog engages, I won't be deterred. I relish change.

10. **Open the Door of the Unknown**: The old does not always go away without a fight, without questioning and without protest. "Do you know what you're doing? Do you really want to try that? Have you lost your mind? You know you haven't done that before; been there before; you could be making a wrong decision." I acknowledge my feelings, my fears, but I still forge ahead, not willing to close the door to the possibilities. I refuse not to allow myself to try. I might fail, but after all, I have the where-with-all to deal with failure too. I open the door of the unknown and go inside knowing I have the ability to deal with whatever I am greeted with.
11. **Dreams:** Following your dream and heart can be quite risky, but *not* following them can be riskier.
12. **Join the Parade**: I won't sit passively by, watching others who have joined the parade: the parade of self-employment, confident living, living their dreams or building the life they've always envisioned for themselves instead of just existing.
13. **Mistakes?** Making a mistake does not mean staying on the sidelines and not taking a chance again. Edison didn't name 10,000 failures a mountain of mistakes, but knew it was the key to finding what *did* work on his road of discovery in inventing the light bulb. I'm glad he had the self-discipline and the inner fortitude to keep going past 9,999 and to take another chance or perhaps I'd be journaling by candlelight.
14. **Lessons in Failures:** Our failures, our ability to take chances and move beyond our comfort zone arm us with the knowledge of what we like and don't like; what we want to do and don't want to do. Taking chances builds the foundation for growth and education.

15. **Actions:** I will not merely talk about good ideas, as most men do, but I will follow through with plans, proposals and actions. I will fill the knowing-doing gap.
16. **Creativity:** I will believe in my ideas and in my ability to create even when others don't. I will not belittle my ability to create but know that when my ideas are rejected, perhaps I presented them to someone not capable of partnering with me for the birthing of the idea during this season.
17. **Ignore Feelings and Act**: I will act on my ideas, regardless of my feelings. Feel the fear and act anyway (this would make for a good book title!).
18. **Intelligence and Gifts**: My gifts will make room for me before great men. (Proverbs 18:16 KJV)
19. **Stretching My Wings:** I have wasted too many years abiding in "the narrowest nest in the corner, my wings pressing close to my side." It really is time to *stretch my wings*.
20. **Leaving:** I've always known I didn't belong in a 9-to-5 job. It's challenging leaving a job behind, your colleagues behind, and a steady paycheck behind, but I must listen to my inner-voice telling me it's time to go in a different direction. I feel stifled. I feel like I'm going to choke on routine, the system, the security, the sameness, the lack of control about when I'm free to go to the bathroom, about being allowed only a 15-minute lunch break. I hate being in the employment fishbowl.
21. **Struggling:** Why am I struggling with guilt, when I hear my neighbors head to work in the morning? Guilt of being too free? Am I feeling deserving of controlling more of my life, getting rid of the unpleasantness and stress the job was causing me? Sometimes I feel isolated; at other times, I feel

that perhaps I am not being productive enough. A smorgasbord of feelings hits me, filling me with self-doubt. I'm working from home; why doesn't that seem like enough? Others are free to control their time, so why not me?

22. **Questioning Myself:** There's that tugging reminder that my dad worked one job for forty years while also working his part-time job for another 25 years, and he labeled my obsession for breaking away from a 9-to-5 job as laziness. Is it really the quality of life as well as the quantity? Isn't it about doing more than accumulating, but enjoying the "what and how" of our accumulation?

23. **My True Source:** God is my source. God is my husband. God supplies my needs according to His riches in glory. I need to put my money where my mouth is. Otherwise, do I really believe that, or am I just giving lip service to it? Is a job really my source, foundation and supplier? People ask me constantly what I am going to do when my sabbatical is up. Will I return to a job that I find restricting for this season of my life?

24. **Fighting Discouragement**: Today my inner voice is telling me to quit, not to return to work in the fall. The voices of friends and family members are warning me to proceed with caution. I know the season for this job has ended, and it's difficult for me to continue going back.

    God has promised to give me the desires of my heart; therefore, God, please help me find the courage and resources to leave.

25. **Know Thyself**: A successful life means knowing yourself well, being a student of you; you are with yourself all the time. If anyone knows you through and through, your likes and dislikes, it should be you.

Do you have a love relationship with yourself? Do you feel deserving and worthy? Have you realized that the key to your happiness rests on you and not on others, not even on your spouse? Do you know what makes you happy, truly happy?

Are you willing to allocate resources, time and money to treat yourself the way you deserve to be treated? Spiritually, do you realize you are a king's daughter?

26. **Life under Exploration**: God has promised me abundant life, and I deserve abundant life. I deserve to live a life that is fulfilling to me career-wise (at work) and personally (at home).

27. **Tuning into My Spirit**: When I am anxious, unhappy, and frustrated, I know why. I only have to look inside and be brutally honest with myself and to be honest with God. He knows my thoughts from afar. I can't hide from Him, nor can I hide from myself. God's wisdom and counsel is available to me. I can use these tools to solve problems. I can use these tools when I am seeking an answer.

28. **Deserving**: I will feel and act deserving. Acting deserving means asking, moving through life confidently, and moving through life expecting to win, with high expectations.

29. **No Lack**: The things that I need in life emotionally, physically, spiritually and materially will be there for me and are there for me now. God has given me all things that pertain to life and godliness (2 Peter 1:3 KJV). I can step into my future confidently. I can step into my future with the favor of God and with assurance that I will have abundance in all aspects of my life.

30. **The Way:** The way for me is already made. The path and all that I need on the journey is already there. There are times

the way seems hidden by obstacles, challenges, rejections, and my own lack of assurance, but the way is there nonetheless.

31. **Victorious:** I am a winner; I am an overcomer in all aspects of my life (2 Corinthians 2:14 KJV). I am victorious. I don't have to act wimpy or act or talk like a grasshopper. I am a giant killer.
32. **Winning Breeds Winning**: I find the courage to win by winning.
33. **Expectations:** I have high expectations and expect to win.
34. **In Pursuit of Goals**: I go after my goals and enlist the help of others with high expectations and an attitude that portrays I am a winner and that I expect to win.
35. **Courage:** Others find the courage to win by my winning.
36. **Confidence:** I am confident, courageous, and capable.
37. **Winning in Action:** I am a role model for my children and others. I am an example of how winners persist in winning. I show them how winners act when they are fighting to win, and when they have won.
38. **The Vision**: I envision or see myself winning before I've won.
39. **Allow Others to Grow:** I allow others their unique chance to grow. I won't burden myself in this life by being judgmental, by being critical because they are seemingly struggling in an area of life. Being critical and judgmental is actual being prideful and arrogant. When I see someone else struggling, instead I will choose to whisper a prayer for him or her.
40. **Avoid Quicksand**: I won't get caught up in the quicksand of life. The quicksand of bad habits, negative thoughts, envy or paralyzing fear.

41. **Others' Opinions**: What others may think about me is not my problem. Worrying about how others see me or about their opinion of me is not conducive to my mental and emotional health and well-being. I have chosen not to make others opinions my concern; otherwise, it becomes baggage that I choose not to carry through this life. As the adage goes: It's not my business what you think of me; it is my business what I think of you.
42. **Mentors:** When the student is ready, the teacher will come. As I travel down my growth and learning paths, God will provide fellow travelers with the willingness to stop and share the lessons I need; I will also share with them. Although there may be times I feel alone, I am really never alone.
43. **Focus on Strengths**: I will look at what I have and not at what I don't have. I will look at my capabilities instead of my inabilities.
44. **Gratefulness:** I will continue to count my blessings.
45. **Obstacles**: Challenges to my creative spirit and obstacles as I travel along the way are just opportunities to grow and enhance my problem-solving skills.
46. **Helping Others:** I will not be too busy to help others who ask for directions as they make their journey.
47. **Embracing My Skills:** I will not devalue my skills.
48. **Past Victories:** I will not devalue my past successes and will look at them for encouragement for success in my future projects.
49. **Gathering Information:** I will take time to think and plan my journey and to build my knowledge and resources.
50. **Help:** When I feel I am lost, I will take time to ask someone to give me directions.

51. **Ditch the Baggage:** I will refuse to take the baggage of lost time, lost position, rejection, misunderstandings and unforgiveness with me.
52. **Meditate and Reflect:** I will not be so busy that I miss the simple things in life. I will slow down, sharpen my ax, and take time to meditate, think, pray and analyze.
53. **Not Fearing Failure:** There are some lessons I will learn by failing, by not being perfect, by not doing things correctly the first time. I will think of my failures as opportunities to reevaluate, educate and grow.
54. **Risks**: I will take plenty of risks. I recognize that taking risks is part of the game-plan for winning. "Nothing ventured, nothing gained" is trite but true.
55. **Confidence**: I will be confident.
56. **Actions:** I will act confidently.
57. **Inner Dialog:** I will give myself messages; my inner conversation will help build my confidence. I will not ignore my inner-voice; I will make it an ally and a friend. Because it seems silent to the world, I will not underestimate its importance.
58. **Learning the Success of Others:** I will not envy others who are excelling and stretching their wings. I will study their successes to drink in lessons on self-determination, courage, persistence and other character strengths.
59. **Eliminate the Need for Perfection**: Putting the necessity on myself to be perfect is not realistic. Perfect people don't exist. However, I will always put expectations on myself to be the best I can be where I am spiritually and emotionally and according to the knowledge I have or have access to.
60. **Growth, a Never-Ending Path**: I will never stop growing.

61. **Be Courageous**: I will be courageous and grow. As Joshua 1:8 (KJV) says, "Be strong and of a good courage…"
62. **Attitude:** I realize my attitude can determine my altitude and greatly impact my efforts to succeed.
63. **The Gift**: I know life is a gracious gift to be unwrapped, used and enjoyed.
64. **Don't Quit**: I won't give myself the option to back down because I feel fear or feel uncomfortable.
65. **Be Uncomfortable**: I forge ahead despite my uncomfortable feelings. Leaving my comfort zone can be uncomfortable. I refuse to let those feelings interfere with my progress and my ability to stretch and reach for more and succeed.
66. **Defining Success**: I define what success means to me. I am careful not to put my ladder of achievement against the wrong wall. But when I feel I am climbing the wrong wall, I give myself permission to move my ladder to a different wall or to make a goal U-turn. I re-aim.
67. **Search for Knowledge**: Not knowing all I need to know about a subject, issue, or field will not thwart my desire and commitment to forge ahead. As I move down the path, I will become wiser, stronger and more capable.
68. **Challenges**: There are lessons in the challenging moments of life. Just as people have to mine diamonds, I must look to mine the gems out of the dark places of my life. The diamond, after all, was made through years of pressures. What are the pressures, stresses and challenges making me into? Only I can determine this, because the attitude I choose to adopt, during trials and challenges, is a personal decision. Circumstances are not always within my control, but attitudes are.

69. **Preparation:** I will prepare for success because I know it is coming. I will read, think, act and work towards the moment, knowing it will soon knock at my door. If it does not knock at my door, I am prepared to leave my comfort zone and go out and pursue the success I have prepared for.
70. **Not Fearing Success**: I will not fear success when it arrives. Success might bring with it responsibilities, hard work and other unexpected challenges, but I will say a hearty hello when it arrives and know I will be able to handle it. As one well-known pastor Bishop T.D. Jakes asks, "Can you stand to be blessed?" Yes, I can.
71. **Keep Moving Forward**: I will never forget what I've learned as I've grown. I will continue to apply the lessons.
72. **Enjoy the New:** I will enjoy working and living in the new season of my life. I will use my gifts and talents to benefit myself and others. I will not become stagnant in my life. If I see areas in my life that I need to change, I will tell myself, "You are capable. You are brave. Now: Cry. Try. Pray. Step."

"You are capable of far more than you know. You have to believe that. Stop underestimating yourself."
- Valorie Burton
Life strategist, speaker, author of <u>Successful Women Speak Differently</u>

About the Author

Lucille Usher Freeman taught writing in the Chicago Public Schools and at McCormick Place Corporate offices in Chicago. She has written for various magazines and newspapers including the *Beverly Review, Southtown Economist, Chicago After Dark, Black Elegance,* and the *Chicago Defender.*

Lucille authored *Today My Sister Is Getting Married* and *Silly Caterpillar,* and she co-authored *Stretch Your Wings: Famous Black Quotations for Teens.* She participates in writing conferences throughout the nation and is a professional member of SPAA (Speakers, Publishers, and Authors Association), and STAT (SPAA Theatre & Performing Arts). She has co-written several professionally produced plays: *The Sam Cooke Story: A Change Is Gonna Come; The Teddy Pendergrass Story: Life Is a Song Worth Singing* and *The Jackie Wilson Story: Lonely Teardrops.* Lucille contributed to SPAA's collaboration projects *Mashairi: No Matter Your Circumstances Today, Tomorrow Eagles Will Soar; The Power Within; Overcome!* and *The Seeds of Truth.*

Lucille was selected to attend Stanford University's Professional Publishing Course, and was also chosen for residencies at Ragdale in Lake Forest, Illinois, an artists' community founded to nurture creative professionals.

The author can be contacted at:

P.O. Box 1095
Matteson, IL 60443

or by email at:

freemanlucille@gmail.com

Made in the USA
Columbia, SC
24 October 2020